9ᵀᴴ Grade
SURVIVAL GUIDE

Welcome 9th Graders!

Chris Wardwell

Saint Mary's Press®

Dedication

This book is dedicated to the Basilian Fathers (Congregation of Saint Basil), who educated me for over seventeen years of my life and with whom I have worked for the past nine years. No amount of thanks could ever repay my indebtedness to them. I am forever grateful.

It is also dedicated to my son, Jacob, for taking care of Mom and our dog Delilah when I stayed late at work so many nights to write this book, and to my best friend and wife, Christine, for her patience and support.

 Genuine recycled paper with 10% post-consumer waste. 5125500

The publishing team included Steven C. McGlaun, development editor; Lorraine Kilmartin, reviewer; prepress and manufacturing coordinated by the prepublication and production services departments of Saint Mary's Press.

Interior illustrations by Victoria Shuck.

Printed in the United States of America
ISBN 978-0-88489-966-2

Library of Congress Cataloging-in-Publication Data

Wardwell, Chris.
      9th grade survival guide / Chris Wardwell.
      p. cm.
ISBN 978-0-88489-966-2 (pbk.)
      1. High school students—Conduct of life. 2. High school students—Religious life. 3. Catholic high school students—Conduct of life. 4. Catholic high school students—Religious life. I. Title. II. Title: Ninth grade survival guide.
BJ1661.W325 2007
248.8'3—dc22

2006028022

Author Acknowledgments

Bless the LORD, my soul; do not forget all the gifts of God.

(Psalm 103:2, NAB)

So many people deserve my gratitude, but a few need some special recognition here.

Thank you to the teachers of Saint Thomas High School, both past and present, for their dedication to educating young men, especially Joe Zarantonello and West Cosgrove, who continue to inspire me today.

Thank you to all the students who offered their expert advice—especially Caitlin Bambenek, Rory Biesanz, Ben Blanton, Evan Henke, Walker Parkhill, and Emily Sharpe—and helped with research or offered their generous criticism of the first drafts. Also, thank you to my friend Amy Schmidt for her help with this project.

Thank you to all my classmates and teachers at Saint Mary's University of Minnesota, especially Dr. Greg Sobolewski, Sandy Iwanski, and Fr. Tim Backous.

Thank you to all my friends who cheered for me as I wrote this book. They are too numerous to name. Also, a big thanks goes to my family for all their love and support, especially my in-laws, Donald and Rhonda Sweeney; my sister-in-law, Jennifer Sweeney; my brother, Joby Wardwell; my dad, Joe Wardwell; and my mom, Betty Wardwell. Many thanks to my extended family members Stephen, Lisa, Sarah, and Hannah Ondak.

My final and biggest thanks goes to Steven McGlaun, my friend of many years and the editor of this book. Many people asked me how I got the idea for this book. It was very easy—Steven called me up and said, "Hey, I have an idea for this book." Thanks for your inspiration, patience, suggestions, constructive criticism, encouragement, and your bizarre sense of humor that I enjoy and share with you.

Contents

Foreword

WARNING

Reading this book could make your transition into the high school life easier. Possible side effects include, but are not limited to, the following:

- standing out among your classmates due to increased self-confidence
- the ability to cope with and properly address crises when they arise
- effective communication with peers, teachers, and parents
- a deepened faith in God and the gifts he blessed you with

The *9th Grade Survival Guide* is designed to help you on the always exciting and sometimes scary move to high school. Each topic covered in this book was suggested by students just like you. Young men and women entering high school or recently completing their first year of high school met with us and told us all the things "they wish they had known." Their knowledge and experience lie within the pages of this book, where you will read about obstacles, dilemmas, fears, surprises, and numerous other situations you might encounter as you roam the halls of your high school for the first time. Each section presents not only a potential situation but also tips for handling that situation. Some of what you read in these pages will speak directly to what you are feeling, while parts of the book will present information that will come in handy somewhere down the road. Feel free to skip from section to section. As you read, take time to imagine yourself in the situation described and think about how you would respond.

Whether you are entering a private or a public high school, this book can make a valuable contribution to your first year. Not everything you need to know for success in high school is in this book. That would be impossible because the high school years are different for each person. What this book can offer you is a head start and the skills for facing the issues you will encounter. So whether school starts in one week, the first semester is halfway through, or high school is a year away, take advantage of the wisdom this book shares. Have courage and enjoy your high school experience!

NOTES

Part I
Facing Your Fears

"[Jesus] said to his disciples, "Therefore I tell you, do not worry about your life and what you will eat, or about your body and what you will wear. . . . Can any of you by worrying add a moment to your life-span? If even the smallest things are beyond your control, why are you anxious about the rest? If God so clothes the grass in the field . . . , will he not much more provide for you?" (Luke 12:22–28, NAB)

Fearing Fear Itself

In his first inaugural address, United States president Franklin D. Roosevelt said, "The only thing we have to fear is fear itself." That statement might make you wonder whether he was ever a ninth grader in high school! But there is some truth to what he said. The Gospels have many examples of Jesus telling people not to be afraid, and they were in much more dire circumstances than a ninth grader entering high school. In the Scripture passage above, Jesus reminds his disciples that they need not worry because God is with them. Keep these words in mind as you start your first days of high school.

Naming Your Fears

Whether you want to admit it or not, a great deal of fear is generally associated with entering ninth grade. You are taking a step into the unknown, and most people experience a degree of trepidation entering unfamiliar territory. This fear is not unique to you, nor is it unique to the experience of starting high school. If you were walking into an unfamiliar dark room, you might hesitate—a little fearfully—because you do not know what is in there. By turning on the lights, you can see and then deal with whatever is there. Part I is about turning on the lights and eliminating a few fears you might have about high school's unknowns.

High school seniors represent one of the biggest fears that incoming ninth graders have. Questions like "Will they pick on me?" or "Will I get hurt or have to go through embarrassing ordeals during any ninth-grade initiation activities?" may be flooding your mind right now. Do not worry! Yes, sometimes bad things happen, but they are in such a minority that it would be foolish to lose sleep over them. Compare your fear of seniors with some people's worries about flying. These same people have no fear of riding in cars, although statistics show that people have a greater chance of being injured or killed in a car accident than in a plane crash. Worrying about abuse from seniors is similarly useless. You will soon read about some steps you can take to help avoid the wrath of a rare misguided senior.

The high school social scene is also a source of anxiety for newcomers. There is no sugarcoating of this subject on these pages—you will have to make some adjustments—but the experience can be far less traumatic if you handle situations with patience and care.

Most likely your high school has more people, bigger buildings, and a larger campus than your junior high school. Compare the difference to driving in a big city rather than in a suburban neighborhood. You have more roads and more cars to deal with now, and you have to find a parking space at a location where you have never been. And if that weren't bad enough, everyone is driving bumper cars. Yours is a small but efficient economy car, but SUVs surround you. You have only five minutes to get to classes, and the halls resemble five o'clock traffic after every period. Again, try not to worry. This book has ideas to help you around traffic jams so you can get to class on time.

Almost everybody, young and old, has had some version of this dream: you're standing naked in front of a large group of people. This dream reveals the vulnerability everyone feels in certain situations, especially when thrust into a new chapter in their lives. One of the more conscious fears that incoming ninth graders have is similar to the dream: making fools of themselves in public. To be completely honest, making a fool of oneself is almost inevitable. This is true even for adults. It happens to everyone. Hopefully, it will not be a common occurrence for you. What is important to know is how to deal with the situation when you do commit a blunder. Part I includes ways to smooth over the occasional misstep.

What You Will Find in This Section

Part I examines four fears that many incoming ninth graders have about high school. Even if these are not your particular fears, you'll find this section worth reading because you will gain insight into what some of your classmates might go through, to say nothing of the valuable skills you'll learn to help you during your high school career and beyond. Here are the fears that Part I will help you overcome:

- Hazing, Seniors, and Being Picked On
- I Will Not Have Any Friends or Fit In
- I Will Get Lost
- I Will Make a Fool of Myself

As you enter high school life, protect your boundaries, keep safe, and don't be afraid to have some fun.

Hazing, Seniors, and Being Picked On

And what does the LORD require of you
but to do justice, and to love kindness,
and to walk humbly with your God?

(Micah 6:8)

Situation

It's Monday morning, day one of NOW (Ninth-grader Orientation Week, also called Fish Week). Schools have a habit of coming up with cute acronyms, so you had better get used to it. Rumors about this week have been circulating among your classmates. Now it's here. During the first day of school assembly, the principal announced in no uncertain terms that hazing would not be tolerated and that any incident would be dealt with swiftly and severely. Yet you are still nervous.

Ninth graders had been asked to go to the school cafeteria to meet their assigned seniors. Upon entering the school cafeteria, you are handed a goofy-looking beanie with a spinning propeller on top. The word *FISH* is emblazoned on the front. Next, someone hands you the name of the senior who will be responsible for your well-being for the next week. Your pulse quickens. Then a teacher directs you toward a group of students—all of whom stand about three feet taller than you and look like college students. You approach them and call out your senior's name. She steps out, says, "Hey, Fish!" and introduces herself. "Hmm. Okay. So far, so good," you think.

Ninth graders and their assigned seniors sit down to breakfast together, and your senior starts to talk about how much fun you are going to have. Other seniors start laughing. Your mind races; you can only guess about the evil plans they have hatched. An image surfaces in your mind's eye. In it, the doctor tells your parents, "I'm sorry, but we could not remove all the confetti and toilet paper from your child's face because they used hot tar as an adhesive." No, this just cannot be! As you focus again on the room, you see a fellow ninth grader being forced to stand on one of the tables. Oh, no. The torture is beginning. Oh, the humiliation. The seniors laugh as that poor ninth grader sings the school fight song. Why, Lord, why? When your classmate finishes the song, the seniors pat him on the back and continue eating. Uh, hold on. Where was the inhumane torture? the vicious cruelty? All he had to do was sing a song. That was not so bad!

All through breakfast, seniors make their ninth graders sing. One boy sings the latest hit from one of the pop divas. You look across the room at a friend. Obviously under the direction of his senior, your friend approaches a coach to ask permission to untie the coach's shoes and then tie them again. The coach laughs and allows the ninth grader to do the deed. All around you is silliness. Some ninth graders dance under the direction of seniors while others croon awful renditions of songs only your parents could like. The seniors are having a ball. You also notice one more interesting thing—the ninth graders are also having a lot of fun.

Not to be left out, your senior invites you to stand on the table to belt out a song from the past. It's a classic hit to which everyone knows the words, so some of the other seniors get their charges to join in. All together, loud and proud, you sing, "I'm a little teapot, short and stout. / Here is my handle; here is my spout. . . ." Embarrassing? Maybe a little, but you just might be surprised to find the experience more fun than fear.

After breakfast, the principal addresses the students and announces Fish Week activities such as Bobbing for Bananas (do they float?), Dress Your Fish Day, Senior-Fish Karaoke Duos, and other goings-on that sound . . . well, kind of fun. The principal also goes over the guidelines for Fish Week and reminds the seniors of what the school considers appropriate behavior. He reassures the ninth graders that they are not required to participate in any event they are uncomfortable with, but he also encourages them to have fun.

How to Handle the Situation

One of your greatest fears about high school is likely to be hazing. Many ninth graders enter high school fearing what upperclassmen will do to them. Put your mind at ease because in most high schools, hazing is a myth, not a reality. If hazing does occur, it is not treated lightly. Your safety and well-being is the first concern of your school's faculty and staff.

Despite these assurances, you might continue to have reservations because of headlines like "Students Stunned by Senior Stunt " or perhaps "Frenzied Freshmen Found Fleeing Freemont High"? Beyond their bad alliteration, these headlines point to some inappropriate activity that goes on in high schools today. Television news in August inevitably contains stories about yet another hazing incident that resulted in the death or serious injury of a student. Though these events are tragic and should not be tolerated, it bears repeating that they are not the norm—especially in Catholic high schools. Bullying does not have a place on the list of Christlike behaviors Catholic schools work hard to instill in their students. Despite the media exposure these events attract, the majority of high school initiation activities do not result in fatalities or serious injury. Most attempts at injury are directed at your ego, and the weapons usually include making you wear silly hats or your grandmother's clothing.

Ninth-grade initiation should be a fun time for all, but headlines and rumors often inflate the worries of many high school newcomers. To ease your worries, here are some helpful hints to hedge the horror of hazing.

Participate only in school-sanctioned activities.

- If a senior tells you that he or she is going to take you an initiation event not organized by the school, say no. Do not go. Period.

Respect yourself.

- Involve yourself only in activities that will make you and those who love you proud.
- Remember that your being new to a school does not give anybody permission to mistreat you.
- Sometimes a senior steps across the line. If this happens, tell a school administrator about it. Do this not only for yourself but also for other students who might be going through the same experience, as well as for future students who won't have to address the problem because you were brave enough to stand up against it.

 Do your research.

- Knowledge can reduce your anxiety.
- Ask friends or the siblings of friends about their ninth-grade experiences. Events such as ninth-grade initiation are usually school traditions that have not altered. Most likely you will go through initiation rituals similar to those of most ninth graders in recent years.
- Check out the school's policy on hazing.
- Ask a school administrator about past initiations. Did any serious hazing incidents occur? If so, how are they being prevented now?
- If possible, find out the plans for this year's school-sanctioned initiations.

⚠ Be clear with your senior.

- In many schools, each new student is assigned a senior who is called and considered that student's senior (or senior sister or brother). Those with a really warped sense of humor call this person your senior buddy.
- If you are asked to do something with which you are uncomfortable, tell your senior in no uncertain terms that you will not do it. Don't go along in hopes that your senior is joking or in fear that you will find yourself covered in some awful-smelling substance that only comes off with that slimy blue stuff your dad uses to clean his hands after working on the car.

⚠ Have a sense of humor.

- Your entry into high school should be fun. Maintain healthy boundaries, but feel free to jump in and be silly. Willingness to be the brunt of a good-natured joke can make the year a lot more fun for both your senior and you.
- If you show some willingness to do the silly things you are comfortable with, you and your senior will probably have a lot more fun. But if you do not feel comfortable with an activity, DO NOT DO IT!

⚠ Hazing is never appropriate.

- The hazing of a new member of a team, club, or other group is not acceptable. Anything that degrades a person or places a person in physical or emotional danger is not something to be tolerated. If you feel that hazing is occurring or is likely to happen, talk to a coach or a club sponsor. If you are not satisfied with the response, talk to the principal, a counselor, or your parents. Your safety should be your first concern.

Try not to worry!

- Seniors are just three years away from being ninth graders themselves. They remember what it was like. Though they might not want to admit it, they usually have some sympathy for your situation.
- Most initiation activities are fun and enjoyable. If you are clear about your boundaries and participate only in school-sponsored events, very little will deserve your worry.

I Will Not Have Any Friends or Fit In

A faithful friend is a sturdy shelter;
    he who finds one finds a treasure.
A faithful friend is beyond price,
    no sum can balance his worth.

(Sirach 6:14–15)

Situation

It's time for lunch on your first day of school. You make your way across campus toward the cafeteria. As you cross the courtyard, you notice several groups of students sitting outside. You don't know any of them. As you enter the cafeteria, you scope out the scene. Looking to the right, you see no one from your old school. Looking to the left, you still cannot locate a single soul who looks even vaguely familiar.

You decide to head toward the lunch line, realizing that if you were to continue standing at the cafeteria door looking around for a friend, you would look like the loneliest geek on campus. Besides, the lunch line will provide needed time to scan the locale and map out a plan of action. It might even offer the opportunity to meet someone new.

As you slowly stagger forward, you notice another lonely line-dweller behind you. You start to think out loud, casually debating the menu offerings by saying,

"The pizza seems a tawdry attempt at southern Italian authenticity, while the Salisbury steak with macaroni and cheese appears to be an unpretentious and hearty offering, don't you think?" Your companion in line gives you a confused look and takes several cautious steps away.

After this embarrassing attempt to impress your neighbor fails miserably, you look around the room and plan how you will maneuver your way around and avoid sitting next to the (insert appropriate group name here) while at the same time placing yourself at the coolest table where you will meet your best friend for life. As you check out at the cash register, the situation looks hopeless.

You walk quickly away from the lunch line and try to look as though you know where you are going. You stride swiftly and confidently, but it soon becomes apparent that you are circling aimlessly around the cafeteria. After the fourth revolution, the sophomores begin to place bets on the total number of times you will circumnavigate the school's dining establishment.

You are finally driven outside to find a bench, convinced you will eat lunch alone for the entire four years of high school. "I'll be okay," you tell your miserable self. "I'll just use my lunch period to read a book or get my homework done early." You begin to delude yourself with demented notions about the virtues of a solitary life. You are a sad and pathetic excuse for a teenager.

It does not have to be this way.

How to Handle the Situation

In addition to the stress of adjusting to new teachers, tougher classes, and new surroundings, ninth graders also have to deal with the daunting task of finding their way in a new social environment. Expectations are high, quite often too high, and the idea of making new friends can be intimidating.

When it comes to the high school social scene, some people think that when they enter high school, life will become like one of those reality television shows where the language is bleeped out so much that it is difficult to follow the plot line. In fact, some good young leaders arise who will usually help blaze the trail through high school. You can be one of them.

An astute ninth grader might also notice that high school seniors tend to be quite accepting of one another—or at least more accepting than are their younger schoolmates. As the members of a class approach the end of their high school careers, they seem to appreciate one another, especially their differences. Wouldn't it be great to get a head start on that?

Making friends will not be difficult, but it might require a little effort on your part. While you are finding and fostering friendships, don't forget to flash back to the following fine formulas.

Get involved in extracurricular activities.

- Join a sport, a club, the student council, a foreign language organization, or one of the many other groups on campus. Membership in a group is a great way to meet people with the same interests.

- Try something that you might not at first consider, such as cross-country skiing or the movie critics group. Joining such groups is a great way to branch out and meet people outside your regular gang.

 ## Try to meet a lot of different kinds of people.

- High school is a great time to broaden your horizons. Catholic high schools usually have more students than the Catholic junior highs that many students previously attended. The experience is also new for those who went to public grade schools. The point is that high school is full of people with varying backgrounds and experiences who are interesting and fun to be around. You might be surprised by whom you enjoy being around.

 ## Do not worry about what other people think.

- Telling someone not to worry about what other people think is sometimes like telling someone in the path of a tornado not to worry about the wind. You can talk until you are blue in the face, but people are still going to worry. Nonetheless, you can do things to lessen the impact of your peers' influence on your life.
- Some people do not always get along with others. It is unreasonable to expect that all your friends will like

one another. Hang around the people you want to hang around with.

- Be self-assured enough not to be swayed by public opinion.
- Do not check the polls. What if Juliet had not considered Romeo because he was not popular among her friends? They would never have gotten together and . . . uh . . . well . . . okay . . . she would not have died. But while true, that's not the point.

You have nothing to prove among true friends.

- Don't you hate it when your parents say, "If he really were your friend, you wouldn't have to prove anything to him"? Well, the worst part is that it is true. If being someone's friend includes being pressured into doing something you don't think is right, just don't do it. True friendship will not put you in that situation. You will also come to regret your participation. (Don't you hate it when your mom and dad are right?)
- You might think that rejection by a particular group of people will sound the death toll for your social life. Not true. If you make the effort, you will always be able to find friends who accept you for who you are.

Your old friends will make new friends too.

- Making new friends is exiciting, but remember that your old friends will be doing the same. Keep a check on your jealousy.

- Just because your old friends hang out with someone you do not really like is no reason to end your friendship. You do not have to become buddy-buddy with the new person in order to remain friends with your old friends.

Choose your friends wisely.

- Peer pressure is a lowdown, dirty thing. Teenagers tend to deny its power, but secretly they all know the lure of social acceptance and the deep fear of being excluded. Putting yourself in the company of people who do not live by the same moral code that you do can put you dead-center in a situation you will most likely regret. Avoid it.
- Surround yourself with people who are positive, honest, and supportive of you. You do not need put-downs, insults, and a negative worldview in the midst of so many changes in your life.
- Many lifelong friendships begin in high school. For some reason, this seems to be more true for friends who met in Catholic schools. Something about the environment encourages these relationships. Maybe the reason is the sense of family that Catholic schools work hard to encourage among students and faculty. Whatever the reason, make sure you take advantage of it. Find good friends and keep them.

Everyone gets lost once in a while.

I Will Get Lost

The Israelites said to Moses, "We are perishing; we are lost, all of us are lost!" (Numbers 17:12)

Situation

You look at the clock. The minute hand is about to fall as the teacher wraps up a lecture on expectations for the fall-semester biology class. You subtly fill your backpack a minute or so early. A drop of sweat slowly trickles down your forehead just . . . as . . . the . . . period . . . bell . . . RINGS!

And you're off. From the strategically located seat chosen for its proximity to the exit, you run toward the door. You are the first out of the classroom. Yes! Off you go, down the hallways of Saint Eusebius High School Raceway. You speed around the corner, just missing the new French teacher, who is balancing a full cup of hot coffee on her briefcase. You duck under the backpack of a varsity lineman to avoid catching a senior's eye. In just under two minutes, you've arrived halfway across campus to your locker. You have one minute to pack up your books and make it to algebra on the other side of the school. There, it is rumored, the teacher has an intense distaste for tardiness. You look at your watch. Yes! Time is on your side and the hallways are thinning out, allowing you more room to maneuver between your peers. You look at the school map your mother made, then you fold it up and stick in your back pocket (okay, maybe she was right). You hop over a fellow ninth grader bending over to tie his shoe. You dodge the oncoming traffic by jumping up and turning yourself sideways between two pedestrians while still maintaining forward motion. The hallways become less and less populated, signaling the approaching sound of the tardy bell. Your destination has got to be just around the next corner. You turn, reach for the door, and step into the classroom at the sound of the bell. Ah, you did it! You are flooded with relief and the sense of a job well done. When you look up, you find a class full of juniors and a sweet, elderly history teacher asking if you are lost. Lost!? No, it can't be . . . the strategic seat location . . . the map . . . the plans . . . the swift footwork in the hallways . . .

How to Handle the Situation

Navigating unfamiliar surroundings is a challenge for anyone at any age. If you look around, you will notice that other people are also trying to figure out where they are and where they should be. New teachers and staff members as well as transfer students in their sophomore, junior, or senior years have the same problems.

These difficulties can be diminished, if not eliminated—through preparation. High schools often have a practice run-through for new students during orientation. Teachers open their classrooms and the bells ring as on a regular school day, except that the periods are only long enough for teachers to introduce themselves and answer questions about the location of the students' next classroom. Other teachers and older students stand in hallways to direct the wayward travelers in their search for their next academic abode.

If your school does not have a practice like this, you can do some things on your own. Grab a few friends who will go to the same high school and try the following suggestions.

Walk through your schedule before the first day of school.

- Most schools are open during the summer. Ask the admissions counselor or someone in the main office for permission to acquaint yourself with the campus. You and your friends might even be offered a tour.
- Try to find out where your locker is—or at least its general location. Usually lockers are assigned according to grade level. Ninth-grade lockers will most likely all be in a single location.
- If you get your schedule before the first day of school, visit the school and walk from classroom to classroom, following your schedule as you would during a regular school day. Note any long treks that you will need to make. Can you make them easily in the allotted time?
- Schedule trips to your locker. If you have to go across campus to get to your next class, it is probably not a good time to stop at your locker. Pack up two classes worth of books and avoid the extra stop.

⚠ Keep a map handy.

- Usually the school provides incoming students with a map of the campus. If not, ask for one at the main office. If there is no map, draw one.
- If you are worried about looking foolish, ask yourself whether looking at a map is more foolish than walking in late to class. If you are still worried, reduce your map on a copier so it is not so obvious, or just put it inside a binder. No one will notice.

⚠ Know how the buildings are arranged.

- Most classrooms are numbered in an organized manner. For example, each room number might have four digits. The first digit usually indicates the number of the building. The second digit specifies the floor level. The remaining two digits identify the room. Room 2217, then, is located in the second building (first digit), on the second floor (second digit). Take a minute and figure out how the rooms in your school are numbered.
- High schools are also often arranged by academic departments. For example, all the science classes are usually located in the same building or hall, while the English classes are held in another. This isn't always true because some instructors teach in both departments, yet have only one classroom. By remembering the locations of these main departments, you at least narrow down the possibilities.

Ask for help.

- Teachers should always be willing to help you, that is, if they aren't also new to the school. Older students might be good sources of information. If you are too embarrassed to ask them, check with a fellow ninth grader. You will often share the same teachers and they may have the same teacher and classroom, just at a different time.
- The maintenance workers are your friends. No one knows the campus better than they do. They are usually more than happy to assist you.
- Drop into the counselors' office, the library, or the main office if they are nearby. Someone there is bound to be able to help you.

Do not worry!

- Your teachers will probably be forgiving if you are late the first few days. They know that you are still learning your new environment. They usually have a short grace period regarding tardiness. But make sure you do not try to take advantage of their kindness!
- Not knowing where you are is a temporary condition that is easily solved. By the end of the first week, you should have your schedule down. By the second or third week, you will probably know the campus very well.

I Will Make a Fool of Myself

Do not deceive yourselves. If you think that you are wise in this age, you should become fools so that you may become wise. For the wisdom of this world is foolishness with God. (1 Corinthians 3:18–19)

Situation

This is it—the night of the first dance of your ninth-grade year. You shower, brush your teeth, and spray a little breath freshener. You pick out your nicest clothes, put them on, and check yourself in the mirror so many times that your little brother starts to make fun of you. Nonetheless, you continue because you do not want one thing out of place. This is your night.

You feel like you have prepared well for the evening. Last week you rented the DVD showing you how to dance the latest urban-pop-mambo-hip-hop-salsa-groove-cardio-funk-swing, but of course you didn't tell anyone about that. You want people to think that you were born knowing how to dance that way. You're a natural, of course!

Your mom drops you off a block away from school so you can walk the rest of the way and make your grand and fashionably late entrance. You walk into the gymnasium, ready for the love and adoration of your peers. The music is loud. You nod to a friend in the distance as you stroll over to check out the hors d'oeuvres. You decide against the Cheetos, fearing they might clash with your breath freshener, not to mention that cheesy-lip look that can be such a turn-off.

You determine that the dance floor is ready for you. You look over and see that special someone you have had your eye on. You have also noticed this person looking at you in the hallway on your way to biology class. Your souls connect and the next thing you know, you are on the floor shaking your body in time. Your hair moves with the rhythm but falls back into place, just like in the commercials on television. The lights flash as the deejay spins the hits.

Then out of nowhere you hear laughter. You turn around to see what is going on. Maybe it is the drama teacher, Mr. Green. You had heard that he thought of himself as quite the talented break-dancer who was not shy when it came to displaying his imagined talents. Or maybe it is the old music teacher dancing with Father Schwenzer, the principal who won a few jitterbug contests in his younger years.

You turn around but do not see anything funny. You notice a crowd looking at you. But why? They are all laughing. As you try to figure it out, your partner starts to laugh too. "What's going on?" you think. "Is it my clothes? my hair? Did my clothes rip?" Your mind races. "Is it my dancing? Did someone stick a sign on my back?" Dreadful thoughts spin out of control. "Is there something hanging out of my nose? Why are they laughing at me?"

How to Handle the Situation

Looking like a fool happens to everyone. Presidents, teachers, movie stars, your friends, your parents . . . everyone looked like a fool of at some time and in one way or another. What separates the eternal fool from the temporary fool is how each handles the situation. It is a pleasure to present these particular propositions on how to prudently preside over the public faux pas.

Laugh at your own blunders.

- A surefire way to quiet a classroom full of students laughing at your slipup is to laugh at yourself. The message is loud and clear: "I messed up. I am not perfect, but it is not the end of the world and it is not really a big deal." You will be amazed at how the rest of the class will follow that lead.

- When the word about your gaffe gets around school, someone will inevitably approach you in the lunchroom and try to get a rise out of you by saying something like, "Hey, I heard about (fill in your particular blunder). You are such a dork!" To take the wind right out of this naysayer's sail, try this response: "Yeah, that was a dumb thing to do! I don't know what got into me." Then quickly change the subject.

Do not let it get you down.

- If you get through life without a few first-class goofs, you will be the first human to achieve this. It is amazing how many people have gone on to live successful and happy lives after making fools of themselves. They even somehow learn to look back and see the humor in it too.
- Put the situation into perspective. Of all of the things happening in the world (poverty, war, sickness), is this event really worthy of your anxiety and despair?
- If the event still bothers you, talk to someone you trust right away. Your parents, friends, and teachers have all been in the same position and can offer advice or at least an open ear. If that doesn't help, see the school counselor. It is better to address the issue right away so that it does not linger and keep bothering you.

 Learn from your mistakes.

- Without mistakes, humans would not have learned as much as they have. Something truly positive can come out of a miserable experience, even though it feels like nothing good could ever result from the misery that engulfs you.

 **Try not to pay much attention to public opinion.**

- Public opinion ebbs and flows. The only thing you can count on is that it will change. Only one opinion is important, and that opinion is way past the confines of high school popularity contests. God is the one who should guide your ways and remind you of the important things in life. In the passage at the beginning of this chapter, Saint Paul points out that looking like a fool is not so bad, if it is for the right reasons. God also puts people in their place when they start to think that they are so cool. It is a good thing to remember what real foolishness looks like.

Part II
Things That Might Surprise You

What could surprise you about high school? Well, that all depends. Have you ever watched a scary movie that you had already seen? Even though you knew the villain was going to jump out at the end, did the scene still scare you? High school is similar. You may know a lot about high school life, but you can still be surprised. This is a good time to clear up a few myths.

Myth: I Will Be on My Own

High schools are testing grounds to see whether you will sink or swim in life. Those who sink are sent to the back of the room where they stay for the rest of the year. The teacher eventually forgets their names and ceases grading their tests.

Not true. Catholic high schools have many opportunities for you to get help. The last thing they want you to do is sink. In fact, many times the school will start throwing life preservers to you before you even know your boat is leaking.

Myth: Catholic High Schools Are Incredibly Difficult

Catholic schools are known to be so difficult that most colleges do not even require Catholic school graduates to take classes. They just give them diplomas and send them straight to graduate school to get their masters' degrees.

Not true. Although Catholic schools are known for their superior academic standards, they generally do not accept students who they feel cannot handle the work. As long as you are focused and have your priorities straight, you can succeed in a Catholic high school. As with any other school, you will find some classes difficult, but you might be surprised to find a few easy ones too.

Myth: Catholic Schools Do Not Have Extracurricular Activities

Because the students spend all their studying and going to Mass—or going to confession for not studying and going to Mass—they do not have time to play sports or have fun.

Not true. Although Catholic high schools might not have the resources to provide as many extracurricular activities as public schools do, there is still no lack of opportunity for you to get involved and have a lot of fun. You might be surprised to find out how many chances you will have to interact with your friends outside of class.

What You Will Find in This Section

In this section, we will look at four aspects of Catholic high school life that just might surprise you. Even if you are not that surprised, you'll still find a lot of good information in the following sections:

- So Many Options, So Little Time
- You Are Not Alone
- High School: Easier Than You Think
- Take Advantage of Help

September

9 MONDAY

6:00-6:05 get up and shower
6:05-6:15 study for the MATH TEST
6:10-6:30 get dressed
6:25 breakfast
6:30 - yearbook meeting at school
7:30-11:30 CLASSES !!!
11:30-12:15 lunch; write English essay!!
    look for my report — in my locker?

12:15-2:30 classes (again!)
2:30-3:30 track practice   RUN! RUN! RUN!
3:25-4:05 volunteer at Senior Center
4:15- 4:45 Piano lesson ♪ ♪ ♪ (practice!)

4:45 — meet JUDITH at the Mall!

5:30 walk Harold the dog
6:00 Dinner
6:15 - 7:15 work on biology paper
7:30-9:00 Bible study at Meg's
        BRING FOOD
later — call Pam, finish biology paper
    before bed

When you do too much, you end up doing nothing very well.

So Many Options, So Little Time

My child, test yourself while you live;
  see what is bad for you and do not give in to it.
For not everything is good for everyone,
  and no one enjoys everything.
Do not be greedy for every delicacy,
  and do not eat without restraint.

(Sirach 37:27–29)

Situation

Maria was an outgoing ninth grader who was excited to enter this new world of new friends and new surroundings and new adventures and, well, everything was just so . . . uh, well . . . new. So many people had told her that high school was the best four years of their lives that Maria wanted to make the best of high school as well. She had been a good student in elementary school, and she felt confident that she could manage the challenges of high school academics. Even Maria's parents encouraged her to branch out, meet new people, and enjoy herself.

Maria did just that. In her first semester of high school, she successfully ran for student council. She played on the volleyball team. To broaden her horizons, she joined the debate team and then realized that if she joined the Culinary Club, she could learn how to cook and give her hardworking mother a break every now and then at dinnertime. Maria also spent a lot of time on the weekends getting to know her new friends. She met them at football games, and they went out for late-night snacks or spent the night at one another's homes.

Maria noticed that her new teachers seemed to give a lot more homework than her junior high teachers had. "That's okay," Maria thought. "They understand that we need to adjust and meet new people. They won't mind if I turn something in late now and then." She ignored most of her teachers' warnings. She dismissed them, thinking, "I'm sure they are just trying to scare us."

A few weeks into the school year Maria got home late because she stayed after school to attend a student council meeting and then helped her friend build the set for an upcoming musical. When she walked into her house, Maria found her mom and dad sitting at the table. Both had stern looks. A sheet of paper— her first progress report—lay on the table. Ugh! She saw grades on it that she had never seen before. Maria was surprised and embarrassed.

A long discussion and an hour later had Maria out of the Culinary Club (despite her argument that she was doing it "for you, Mom"). She lost the debate with her parents, so Debate Club was also a goner. Her weekend activities were limited to a single event. She could no longer spend the night at her friends' homes, at least not until she brought her grades up to par.

Maria had to give some credit to her parents. They were really not that angry. They seemed frighteningly understanding, as though they had been through it before or something. They said they just wanted to help

Maria focus a little more on her education because that is what school is essentially about.

By the end of the first quarter, Maria had brought her grades back up, but the damage had already been done. Her first-quarter grades were not what she had expected or hoped. Her mom wisely commented that if she learned from the experience, then it was not so bad. Maria felt better and was able to take something positive from the experience.

How to Handle the Situation

Student council. Football. Spanish Club. Debate Club. Cheerleading. Frisbee Club. National Honor Society. Drama. Fellowship of Christian Athletes. Intramural sports. Newspaper. Culinary Club. Band. Volleyball. Cross country. Art Club. Amnesty International. Chess Club. Choir. French Club. Academic Challenge. Dance squad. Respect Life Club. Black Student Union. Yearbook. The Film Critics' Corner. Bowling Club. Campus ministry. Morning announcement group. Model United Nations. Pep band. Retreat team leaders. Web Page Design Club. And the list goes on and on and on. One could keep sufficiently busy in high school without ever attending a class. It would behoove you to be abstemious. (Go get the dictionary; this book isn't going anywhere.) What follows is a little advice for those on the path toward an abstemious lifestyle. (Did you look up abstemious yet? If not, go do it now. What are you waiting for?)

Get involved.

- Joining sports and clubs are great ways to meet people, have fun, and learn something new.
- Participating in extracurricular activities allows you to get to know some adult members of the school community on a different level. You might find out that your theology teacher does not just sit around and talk about the Bible all the time; he plays a pretty mean guitar too. These new relationships with your teachers can also provide you with a good source for advice and direction when you get in a jam—academically or otherwise.

Keep academics your primary focus.

- If you really love all the new clubs and activities, then you need to remember that there are two words you never want to hear: academic probation. Academic probation means that you cannot participate in any extracurricular activities until you are performing at a satisfactory level in your classes. If you do not do the work, you will not be allowed to have the fun.
- You might really love your high school, but if you are not serious about your schoolwork, you might not be allowed to return the next year. Catholic schools are private institutions that do not have to keep you enrolled. Almost all Catholic high schools have waiting lists of people who would love to have the opportunities you have. Don't blow it.

Set boundaries and goals.

- People have different talents and abilities. One person can read a section in a textbook just once and remember every concept on the page, while you might have to read it several times before even the main idea sets in. Similarly, just because your friend can join ten clubs and still make good grades does not mean you can pull it off too. When planning your activities, make sure you do not accept every invitation from your friends, thinking that if they can do it, so can you.
- Make some goals concerning new activities. Look ahead to your four years of high school and make an effort to try at least one new activity each year, or maybe more. How often do you want to try something new?

 ## Get a calendar and use it.

- One of the biggest difficulties ninth graders have is managing their time. Parents usually back off when their kids hit high school (though it probably doesn't feel like it) and allow their teenagers to take more responsibility for their lives. Without a voice hovering over them, new high schoolers can go a little wild when it comes to their schedules.
- Sometimes your mind might not keep track of activities as well as you think it does. A simple way to avoid complications is to keep a calendar for activities. For instance, if you have a test on Thursday and your friends invite you out Tuesday night to watch their basketball

game, you might think, "Sure, I don't have any tests on Wednesday. I can go." What you might forget is that you promised to volunteer to prepare ballots for the student council election Wednesday night, leaving you little time to study. A well-kept calendar can save you a lot of distress and worry.

You Are Not Alone

"I am with you always." (Matthew 28:20)

Situation

The first semester of your ninth-grade year is finished. After years of As and Bs in elementary school, you have successfully managed to get your first F. To add insult to injury, you got the F in your best subject (at least it used to be). This is not to mention the rest of your report card, which also was not worthy of being posted on the refrigerator at home.

Your dreams about high school have taken a nosedive. Things just are not as you thought they would be. Grade school was so much easier. You knew all the people and understood how the system worked. Now everything has changed—new teachers, harder classes, higher expectations, and so on. Your friends have made new friends, but you have not fared as well in that area either. Things are not so smooth at home. Your bad grades have not only made your parents angry, but they have circled the wagons and are hounding you all the time. Every night is the same routine: "Have you finished all your homework?" "Did you study for your test?" "Your grades better improve or you will never even touch the steering wheel of that car!" You just want to scream and tell them that all the nagging is not helping you in the least.

Deep down you know your parents are trying to help. You know that they care about you. Nonetheless, they do not seem to get it. You have had troubles in the past, but just one area of your life was affected, making it easier to handle. Now, the troubles flood every part of your life. One part goes bad and just seeps into the other parts of your life. You are tired of swimming in water that keeps getting deeper. Life seems to be spiraling downward, and you do not know what to do or where to go for help.

How to Handle the Situation

Entering a new high school can be an overwhelming experience for many young people. It doesn't matter whether the school is Catholic, private, or public the changes can overpower even the most determined and sturdy students. When problems arise, you sometimes feel that no one cares. You feel like just another student in this giant school.

Catholic high schools pride themselves on not treating their students like numbers. Each person is a unique and important part of the community. Other schools may not treat you like dirt, but Catholic schools are far more successful in educating young people because of one particular characteristic: a Catholic school is first and foremost a Christian *community.* Notice that this does not say "place of learning" or "educational institute." Your school is first and foremost a community.

In fact, a few decades ago, the Catholic bishops in the United States wrote a document called "To Teach as Jesus Did," in which they said, "As God's plan unfolds in the life of an individual Christian . . . he does not live in isolation from others. . . . In this community one person's problem is everyone's problem and one person's victory is everyone's victory" (pages 6 and 7). Catholic schools are concerned not just with stuffing your brain but with every part of your life. In 1977 the Vatican group that oversees Catholic education wrote, "The Catholic school is committed thus to the development of the whole [person]." (*The Catholic School,* number 35).

So when you are in a Catholic high school and having difficulty in any part of your life, whether it be academic, social, emotional, or spiritual, you can feel confident that you can turn to someone at your school. That person might be the principal, a teacher, a friend, a counselor, a coach, or one of the many other people who care about you. Here are some helpful reminders when you find yourself in a tough spot.

Teachers are there to help you.

- Did you know that most Catholic school teachers are often paid less than teachers who work in public schools, and yet they still choose to work there? They did not get into their line of work because of prestige and money (check out their cars in the teachers' parking lot). Why then do they do it? There are many reasons, but you can count on this one: Catholic school teachers *want* to be there.

- The teachers care about young people. They want to help you. You will find that they are also willing to come in early and stay after school to help you. Ask one and see what happens.
- Because Catholic schools truly care for the whole person and not just about grades, you will also find support when you have personal problems. In your teachers you will often find understanding confidants who are willing to listen and help. You are not alone.

⚠️ Counselors provide support in many different ways.

- If you are having a difficult time with friends, family, or any other aspect of life, school counselors are there to help. They can help you sort out issues, come up with solutions, and find more help for you if needed.
- Sometimes students are afraid that if they tell the counselor something, they will get into trouble. Whether the issue is physical or sexual abuse, drug or alcohol problems, family issues, or any other problem, a counselor's first priority is to make sure students are safe and healthy.
- If you are depressed, it might help you to know that some counselors are licensed professional therapists as well. They are great at helping you get through the dumps. And if your school counselor is not a licensed therapist, he or she will help you find one.

Your parents will help.

- Believe it or not, your parents probably remember what high school was like, and their experience was not that much different from yours. Although it may not seem like it, they will often be sympathetic to your woes because they likely had them too.

- In most cases, your parents are making a sacrifice to send you to a private school. And the sacrifice is not just financial. Most Catholic high school parents also donate their time and talent to the school. If your parents are willing to make such a sacrifice, they almost certainly will help you through whatever problems you have.

God is always there for you.

- Go to Mass. In many high schools, Mass is celebrated right before the school day starts every morning. This essential element of Catholicism expresses the comforting fact that we are not alone—we are in communion with God and one another.

- Go to Reconciliation (aka the sacrament of Penance and Reconciliation, or confession). In this sacrament, a priest can also provide you with guidance and spiritual direction.

- Pray. Go to the school chapel and spend some quiet time alone with God. Speak to Jesus and do not forget to listen.

High School: Easier Than You Think

"Therefore I tell you, do not worry about your life, what you will eat or what you will drink, or about your body, what you will wear. . . . And can any of you by worrying add a single hour to your span of life? . . . But if God so clothes the grass of the field, which is alive today and tomorrow is thrown into the oven, will he not much more clothe you— you of little faith?" (Matthew 6:25,27,30)

Situation

You are preparing for an algebra test scheduled for the Tuesday after a long holiday weekend. But you cannot focus. Your mind is ruminating over the thousand dilemmas that are racing through your head like a movie in fast motion. If someone recorded your thoughts and transcribed them, the result would go something like this: "I hate algebra class, but I have to study for this test because if I don't, then I'm probably going to fail because I didn't turn in my homework last Thursday, and that teacher has it out for me, so he'll probably grade my test harder than anyone else. What is the use? Not only do I hate algebra, but I hate that (fill in name of your current love interest) who wouldn't go to the dance with me next week because of a 'previous engagement.'

Yeah—whatever. Not that I liked (name) all that much anyway. And besides, all those rumors about me liking (name) that much weren't true, because if they were, I'd really be upset right now, and I would obsess over it over and over and over again. But that's not true. I don't really like (name) that much. I think I might even like algebra more than (name) Heck, I even like my algebra teacher more than I like (name) I need to study for this algebra test. I hate algebra. . . ."

Thirty minutes later you are still looking at the same page in your algebra book and have not prepared for your Tuesday test. You have spent the entire thirty minutes worrying about whether this love interest of yours is really interested in you, despite trying (in vain) to convince yourself that you are not really that interested in that person. Then you berate yourself for wasting time: "I can't stand it when I have a test and I waste time sitting here with the book open and . . ." Thirty minutes later your parents walk into your bedroom to find you with your head on your algebra book, fast asleep and drooling onto page 42. Your parents say, "Oh, look how hard our child has been studying!"

How to Handle the Situation

Stop. Breathe in deeply. Breathe some more. Let all thoughts fall away. You need not worry about anything right now. Just for now, everything is okay.

High school can be much easier than you think—a truism about all of life. We bring on much of our anxiety and worry. And when we do, we agonize so much about our worrying that we end up in a vicious cycle that sucks our time and energy away. In the end, what have we accomplished? Nada. Zip. Zilch. Zero.

When things get hectic (and they will), take a step back, relax, and look at the big picture. This technique will often give you some clarity about the situation and allow you to refocus on the most important tasks at hand. Such times are also good for letting go of the little things: school gossip, past mistakes, what other people think of you, and all of your other little worries. Let it all go.

Have you calmed down yet? If so, read the custom-tailored advice that follows.

Don't sweat the small stuff.

- Make a list and prioritize. By writing down everything you need to do, you can evaluate the relative importance of your tasks. Then you can put aside the other less important things. This might allow you a little more breathing room so you can relax and do what you need to do. Remind yourself that you are not ignoring these things—they are on your list and you will get to them when you can. Then pick the most important thing for you to do right now and *just do it.* When you are done, cross it off your list. This will give you some sense of "mission accomplished," even if it is something small.
- Being rejected by a love interest will most likely happen too. It is a part of life that almost everyone experiences.

Survey the married couples you know to find out how many of them were dumped by a previous paramour—probably most of them. You might want to find out how many couples started dating each other in high school—probably not many.

- Keep a daily journal. Write down everything you are worried about. Keep track of your concerns and anxieties. Then after one year, go back and read them. See whether you still have the same worries and anxieties. Chances are your worries and anxieties will have changed. This will help you keep some perspective on your current woes.

- Although at times it seems like it could end your social life, gossip is small stuff. Gossip—whether about you or about someone else—is not deserving of your time and energy. Most is probably not even true anyway. The best way to make gossip go away is to dismiss it quickly and then ignore it. Gossip-mongers find enjoyment in thinking they are getting to you. When they see the gossip does not bother you, their enjoyment ends and the gossip slowly drifts away. Remember that "the truth will make you free" (John 8:32). (See also "Drama! Rumors, Gossip, and Such" on page 107.)

- See for yourself. Talk to teachers, parents, family friends, and other older people to see what they remember about high school. Ask them about their "small stuff" and compare theirs to your situation.

Focus on the big picture.

- Teachers often give their students a syllabus at the beginning of the semester. One of the best things you can do is to look for the part where the teacher tells you how your final grade is calculated. You will then know in what area to focus your efforts. For example, if a teacher counts homework as 40 percent of your grade, you should be sure to complete all your homework on time (good advice, anyway). If 10 percent of your grade is your quiz average and 30 percent is a semester project, consider it wise to devote more of your time and effort to the project.
- Everyone has limited time and energy. What smart students do is focus that time and energy appropriately. For example, after school you might have an extracurricular activity to attend for two hours, then you might travel home and have dinner with your family. After that you might have three or four hours free before bedtime. What is the most important thing for you to do with that free time?

 ## Learn from your mistakes (but don't dwell on them).

- Keep some perspective. One bad grade will not doom you to fail the class. Alone, this bad grade will not keep you from being accepted to a good college nor will it doom you to a life of misery.

- Likewise, getting into trouble will not sentence you to a life of detention and worried looks from people on the street. Acknowledge what you have done, accept the consequences, and strive to do better the next time. (See also "One Mistake Is Not the End of the World" on page 155.)

High school can be a lot easier when you let friends, family, and teachers help.

Take Advantage of Help

"Truly the thing that I fear comes upon me,
   and what I dread befalls me.
I am not at ease, nor am I quiet;
   I have no rest; but trouble comes."

(Job 3:25–26)

Situation

The time is 11:30 on a Sunday night. Your parents have gone to bed, and your older brother, who used to help you with your homework when you really got in a jam, is away at college. You are working on a major biology assignment and cannot figure out the difference between zygotic and gametic meiosis. You cannot call any of your friends because it is too late and you do not want to get them into any trouble. You do not know what to do. In your panic, you begin to feel about the size of the amoeba you are studying. Your life flashes before your eyes. . . .

First, you will fail your biology class. Your parents will throw a fit, and you can kiss your summer goodbye as you sign up for Biology 101 *again!* Meanwhile, your friends are off to the usual hot vacation spots while you are relegated to spend the summer at "Saint Stanislaus Summer School for the Scholastically Challenged."

Abandoned by your friends, you become a social exile, a nomadic wanderer who never sits in the same spot in the cafeteria. You keep to yourself and mumble senseless phrases in the hallways. Soon you wander off campus between periods and disappear into the city, only to be found twenty years later working part time at a fast-food restaurant. Your parents bring you home. You have a blank stare on your face and all you can say is, "Do you want fries with that?" and "I wish I remembered the difference between zygotic and gametic meiosis." This is your legacy—all because you blew that ninth-grade biology assignment. Such a tragedy—and it could have been avoided.

How to Handle the Situation

Surely you are not the first person in the world to ever have problems in school. Remember Albert Einstein's admonition: "Do not worry about your difficulties in Mathematics. I can assure you mine are still greater." And yes, even Albert Einstein failed. At some point, everybody has trouble in school. Either you don't have enough time to finish a project because of work overload from other classes, or sometimes you find the concepts difficult to grasp. It happens to the best students.

The way you handle these difficult jams can make all the difference. Some students stay up until the wee hours of the morning, sustained by caffeinated colas, which allows them to finish all their assignments just in the nick of time (not a great idea). Some students panic and spend most of their time *worrying* about their assignments instead of *working* on them (not good). Some curse the teachers who gave them the work and then blow off all their assignments (*really* not good). Some students evaluate their standings in their various classes and spend most of their time and effort on the one where a good grade is most needed. This is not the best alternative, but you might have to do this sometimes.

The one thing that most students forget to do is talk to the teacher, which is probably the most effective. Who knows what the teacher might do for the student who asks for advice? If the student were to calmly explain the situation to the teacher and ask for advice, that teacher might decide to extend the deadline. Or the teacher might offer to speak to the other teacher about scheduling a conflicting test at a different time or allowing you to take it at a later date. After all their hard work, teachers do not want to put their students in situations where it is difficult to succeed. They really do want to see their students do well.

So when you are approached by anxiety, aggravation, or arduous annoyance, always appeal to the following admirable assortment of advice.

Turn to your teachers.

- Make sure you do not talk to a teacher in the middle of class or at other inopportune times. The time in class should be devoted to the benefit of all students, and the class period usually does not include enough minutes to address individual problems. See teachers before or after school, between classes, in a study hall, or during lunch if they are available. Then they will be able to offer you undivided attention.

- Teachers are almost always willing to come early and stay after school to help you. Ask one and see what happens. If possible, plan ahead and schedule an appointment.

Count on your counselor.

- If you are having problems in a particular academic area, the counselors might be able to arrange specific help for you. They can put you in touch with a tutor if needed.
- If your problems persist despite your constant efforts, you might need to make sure that you do not have any learning disabilities. The counselors are there to guide you through the process.

Family is fundamental.

- Many young people want to assert their independence and do not like relying on their parents for help. It makes them feel like children. As you grow older, you will realize that you will count on their wisdom and judgment for many years to come. Getting help from someone who is knowledgeable is not a sign of weakness, even if that someone is your parents. Try this test: Ask your parents how often they got advice and help from their parents after college. If they are like most people, they turned to your grandparents for advice. Families are supposed to help one another.

- The last thing you want to do is to keep your parents in the dark if you are having problems at school. One nightmare a parent has is that they will think their son or daughter is doing really well in school only to find a D in biology on that child's report card. They will flip out! But if they know that their high school student is having difficulty and is struggling to improve, they are not as shocked by a bad grade (and you might not have to face the shocking punishment either).

Try a tutor.

- Do not be ashamed of needing a tutor. Everyone needs help sometimes. Even though you probably know some guy or girl at your school who seems perfect, that person likely finds *something* difficult. Okay, so they find it difficult to get bad grades—at least that's something. You get the idea. Successful people are humble and smart enough to seek help when they need it. Think about it. Is it better to get help and do well or to suffer silently alone and fail?
- Many Catholic high schools have a National Honor Society that will put you in touch with a really smart senior who can provide tutoring at no cost.
- If you have problems finding a tutor, ask a teacher or a school counselor to help you find one.

NOTES

Part III
Catholic School Confidential

This section specifically addresses aspects unique to the Catholic high school. For those of you who have been in Catholic schools all your life, keep on reading because there are probably a lot of things in this section that you do not know.

You might have seen movies or heard stories about Catholic schools. As with anything else, some are true, while others are pretty far from the truth. The unknown can be stressful, so let's address some misconceptions about Catholic high schools.

Myth: All the Teachers Are Nuns

Catholic school students are all taught by nuns, most of whom are armed with rulers and ready to inflict injury on the knuckles of the first fledgling to step out of line.

Not true. In the past, Catholic schools were staffed mostly by nuns, brothers, and priests, who all were no more or less mean than any other class of human beings. Many religious orders still work in schools, but because the numbers of those called to religious life has declined over the past forty or so years, Catholic schools are now predominantly staffed by lay people (or people who, like your parents, aren't nuns, brothers, or priests). For over 150 years, Catholic schools have been blessed with faithful nuns who selflessly devoted their lives to educating young people like you, but it is also a blessing to have lay people teach.

Myth: Corporal Punishment Is Allowed

Catholic schools are not bound by state and federal laws, allowing them to inflict their own particular brand of persuasive force on their students (aka "the board of education").

Not true. Catholic schools were once renowned for their strict authoritarian style, but today you will often find a healthy balance between maintaining clear boundaries and providing a comfortable atmosphere for learning. For the most part, Catholic schools have to abide by the same laws and regulations that other schools follow. Just as in any other school, hitting and other types of abuse would be reported to the authorities.

Myth: Only Rich Kids Go to Catholic Schools

Catholic schools are havens for rich kids from families who have money to burn.

Not true. The Catholic Church has long been concerned with social justice issues such as poverty, and that concern extends to its schools. The Church's mission states that its schools must not be available for only the wealthy. In fact, most Catholic schools have a great deal of economic and cultural diversity because of the opportunities offered to lower-income families through scholarships and financial aid. In just one classroom, you will most likely find students from the wealthiest as well as the poorest neighborhoods of the community. You probably won't be able to tell which is which.

Really Not That Different

There are many other myths regarding Catholic schools that could be addressed here, but they'll have to wait for another book. On the surface, Catholic schools are not much different from any other school. You've got seven or eight classes a day, a lunch break, teachers, a principal, and a coach in PE who wears the same ugly shorts that the coaches at every other school wear. It should be noted that only about 75 to 80 percent of the students at Catholic schools are Catholic. Many students in your ninth-grade class might be entering a Catholic school for the first time.

What You Will Find in This Section

So what are the differences between a Catholic school and a public school? In this section, we will look at the following four issues you'll encounter in a Catholic school that you probably would not face in a public high school:
- Leading Prayer on a Moment's Notice
- Mass Mysteries: Sitting, Standing, Responding

- What Is Up with These Retreats?
- Bible and Theology 101

Slow down and take time for prayer.

Leading Prayer on a Moment's Notice

"And whenever you pray, do not be like the hypocrites; for they love to stand and pray in the synagogues and at the street corners, so that they may be seen by others. . . . When you are praying, do not heap up empty phrases as the Gentiles do; for they think that they will be heard because of their many words." (Matthew 6:5–7)

Situation

The bell rings and the students move to their desks. The class settles down as your theology teacher, Mrs. Zimbaldi, takes attendance. You notice that she is coughing quite a bit and finding it difficult to speak. As the students silently get ready for the opening prayer, Mrs. Zimbaldi goes to the podium and coughs several more times. Looking a little out of sorts, she motions for you to come to the front of the room. When you arrive, she hoarsely whispers in your ear, "Will you please lead the prayer today?" Not wanting to disappoint her, you nod your head and move to the podium.

You think, "Okay, what does Mrs. Zimbaldi usually do? She usually reads a Bible verse and then offers a brief meditation. Okay, I can do this!"

Mrs. Zimbaldi has taught high school theology for eighteen years and is well known for her inspiring commentaries on the Scriptures. She always makes God's word come alive, and she encourages her students to do the same. This is your moment to make your teacher proud. She will see how you allow the Holy Spirit to work in your life. She will see you shed light on how we can live out Christ's message of peace and love.

You randomly open the Bible. . . . Ah, the Book of Numbers—it rings a vague bell. You begin reading:

> "Then the LORD opened the mouth of the donkey and it said to Balaam, 'What have I done to you, that you have struck me these three times?' Balaam said to the donkey, 'Because you have made a fool of me! I wish I had a sword in my hand! I would kill you right now!' But the donkey said to Balaam, 'Am I not your donkey, which you have ridden all your life to this day? Have I been in the habit of treating you this way?'" (22:28–30)

Your voice trails off into a barely audible mumble as the class begins to laugh.

You catch a glimpse of Mrs. Zimbaldi as she motions you to move on. You decide that it might be best to put down the Bible and just say a brief prayer from your heart. You have had great ideas in the past and now you can let them out. Uh . . . but you cannot remember any right now. Maybe if you just started speaking. You begin, "Heavenly Lord . . . uh, who art in heaven, we love you and want to do things . . . or stuff, um, that is good. But we know that at times, we sometimes don't do those things . . . that are good. So Jesus sent his twelve epistles to the people of Judaism and . . . prayed for the Holy Spirit to live on top of their heads like a bird . . . but not like a bird on your head . . . more like a spirit

. . . uh . . . and let us please win our volleyball game."
Now completely frazzled, you just want this embarrassing
fiasco to end, so you say, "Amen" and make the sign of
the cross so fast that a girl two rows down feels a soft
breeze. You return to your seat, sink low into the comfort
of your desk, and hope you are never called on to pray in
public again.

Should this opportunity ever arise again, it might be
wise to first examine the following options:

Option One. Say the first prayer that comes to mind:
"Rub a dub dub, thanks for the grub. Yea, God!"

Probable Outcome. Although this method is sure to get
you a few laughs, it will also most likely get you a less
than pleasing glare from the teacher and an in-depth
discussion about the importance and reverence of prayer
. . . that or just a trip to the dean's office.

Option Two. Stare blankly at the teacher in terror and
embarrassment until she speaks up and picks someone
else for the duty.

Probable Outcome. More than likely your teacher will
bail you out; however, you will have to wait through the
embarrassment of your classmates' staring at you. Your
teacher will most likely speak with you privately about
giving you "extra help."

Option Three. Start mumbling under your breath while
occasionally blurting out words such as *thou* and *brethren*

and *shall not* so people think you are having some kind of profound spiritual experience.

Probable Outcome. No one will sit next to you during lunch.

How to Handle the Situation

There is another option. One feature you will notice right away in a Catholic high school is that prayer is an essential element in its daily life. We pray at the beginning of the day before announcements. We pray at the beginning of theology class. Some schools even have prayer at the beginning of every class. Sooner or later almost everyone is called upon to lead a prayer. What follows are some helpful hints to avoid panic so that you . . . uh . . . um . . . do not forget to . . . say stuff . . . or something like that. And that you . . . uh . . . do not look like an illiterate fool . . . and stuff like that. You know what I mean?

Begin with the sign of the cross.

Catholics almost always begin prayer with the sign of the cross. Here's how you do it:
- With your right hand, touch the following in this order: forehead, chest, left shoulder, and right shoulder. Here's a quick way to remember: top to bottom, left to right.
- Make sure you don't do it too fast or it will look like you're trying to shoo away flies (definitely not good).

- The sign of the cross is a symbolic gesture expressing that we are Christians and have taken up the way of Jesus as our own—a path of selflessness that includes carrying our own cross.

Know the Our Father.

The Our Father, or the Lord's Prayer, is a prayer that all Christians have in common.

- Catholics usually do not include these words: "For the kingdom, the power and the glory are yours, now and forever" No, they didn't forget the last line. The doxology (that is the fancy high-falutin' name for this part) is included in the Mass. Go ahead and rehearse it a few times without saying this last line. If you've been saying it since you were a child, it'll probably just come out of your mouth anyway. That's okay.
- You may also notice that some versions of the Lord's Prayer say, "Forgive us our trespasses as we forgive those who trespass against us." Another version uses the words *debts* and *debtors* in place of *trespasses* and *trespass.* The message in the line is the same, and that is asking God for forgiveness for your wrongdoings and for the strength to forgive those who have wronged you.

Pretend that you are talking to a friend— because you are.

- Praying is as simple as talking to a friend about what you are thankful for and about what you need. Imagine that God is right next to you, and simply express your needs and gratitude.

- If, however, you are leading prayer for your class, keep in mind that you are offering up the prayer on behalf of everyone present.

Ask a friend to pray for you—a saint!

- One common misconception that people have about Catholics concerns their relationship with saints. Saints are those people who have led exemplary Christian lives and who Catholics believe are now in heaven with God. The misconception is that Catholics pray *to* saints. This is not accurate. It is like this. Have you ever gone through a difficult time and asked someone to pray for you? Catholics do the same with the saints—they ask them to pray for them. At the end of other prayers, the leader will often say the name of a saint, such as Saint Thomas Aquinas. Then everyone else will respond, "Pray for us." Just as Catholics ask their friends to pray for them, they also ask the those in heaven with God to pray for them too.

The Hail Mary is a uniquely Catholic prayer.

- One prayer that is unique to Catholics is the Hail Mary. As the mother of Jesus, Mary holds a special place in the life of Catholics. They look to her as the highest among all the saints, and in this prayer, they ask her to pray for them too.

Get personal in prayer.

- When praying with a group, you often have opportunities to offer up a special short prayer of your own. These are sometimes called personal intentions. For example, the teacher at the beginning of class will ask students to name any personal intentions. Individual students will randomly call out their own special needs or thanksgiving, such as "For my grandmother, who is sick in the hospital, we pray to the Lord." Then the whole class will respond, "Lord, hear our prayer." This is sometimes done at Mass when only a small group is present. Here are some guidelines:

- Be sincere in whatever you say. Do not ever use prayer as a time for a joke. Also, focus on your needs or the needs of others. Pray for *needs,* not *wants.*

- Respect one another's prayer intentions. Assume that everyone else is being sincere when they pray. If someone is not sincere, let the teacher or priest handle it.

- Use prayer positively. Do not pray for the quarterback of the opposing football team to break his leg in practice. Nor is this the time to comment about or insult others: "I would like to pray for this person, who will go unnamed, because she is sitting in this classroom and who stole my boyfriend. I pray that she gets over the guilt she certainly feels—or at least *should* feel because she totally wronged me. . . ."

- Honor the silence. Remember that praying is a two-way street. There is a time to speak and a time to listen. Respect the time for silence in prayer.

Remember that the Mass and prayer are about
getting closer to God.

Mass Mysteries: Sitting, Standing, Responding

"Do this in remembrance of me." (Luke 22:19)

Situation

You're attending a Mass in a Catholic church for the first time. You have seen the movies that show people kneeling in pews and bowing their heads reverently as the priest chants verses in a foreign language. You have heard about Catholics praying to saints, and you imagine being forced to kneel down in front of some statue of a guy you have never heard of and being made to pray to this false god. Your mind is filled with images of being confined to a room as small as a telephone booth, where your deepest, darkest secrets must be revealed to a stranger wearing a white collar. "What do these Catholics do?" you think.

Your class walks to the chapel (or wherever your school has Mass—sometimes it is in an auditorium or gymnasium). The Mass begins and everyone stands as the priest and altar servers process in. After some singing and other words from the priest, you sit down. Later you stand up again. Then you sit down briefly, then stand, and then kneel. Then a quick stand is followed by a short kneel and then a return to standing position. Toward the end of Mass, you notice freestyle events with some people standing and walking to the front, others kneeling, and still others taking advantage of an apparent optional sitting period. The Mass is ended by a full-group stand as the priest and altar servers exit.

Throughout the Mass, you note the ease of the call and response from the priest and the congregation. Everyone seems to know what to say and exactly when to say it. To you, it seems like an awful lot to memorize. You fear having to memorize all of these words. After Mass, a friend asks you about your impressions, and you mention that you were glad the Mass was in English, that you were a little overwhelmed with all the people's responses, and that you felt like you had been to an aerobic workout with all the standing, sitting, and kneeling.

How to Handle the Situation

It is impossible to explain everything about the Mass within the confines of this book, but here is how you can get through this essential element of Catholic life without making a fool of yourself.

 The Mass has several parts.

- The gathering rites are what Catholics do at the beginning of Mass to prepare for the rest of the Mass. The gathering rites include the entrance song, the greeting, and the penitential rite (in which Catholics ask for forgiveness for their sins). This part of the Mass ends with a short prayer from the priest.

- The next part is called the liturgy of the word, which consists of two or three short readings from the Bible and a few other things. Sometimes the psalms are chanted; at other times a song based on the psalms is sung. After the Gospel reading, the priest spends a few minutes connecting the reading to daily life; this is called a homily. The prayers of the faithful— in which the faithful offer up their needs to God—follow.

- Quite often, the most unusual part of the Mass for a non-Catholic is the liturgy of the Eucharist. You might find that it helps to remember that the word *eucharist* means "thanksgiving." What you will hear are mostly prayers of gratitude for all God's blessings. Toward the end of this liturgy, the congregation says the Lord's Prayer. Then they offer one another a sign of peace by shaking hands with those around them. After another short prayer, people begin to process to the front of the church to receive Communion (see more below). When Communion has finished, this part of the Mass concludes with a short prayer.

- The concluding rites include brief announcements, a short blessing from the priest, and a dismissal for all to go out and serve God and one another as Christ did.

 ## The Mass is the central religious practice for Catholics.

- Catholics go to Mass because Jesus commanded at the Last Supper to "[d]o this in remembrance of me" (Luke 22:19). The Mass is a remembrance of Jesus's saving acts, as well as a holy meal, a sacrifice, and a blessing.

- Catholics believe that through the celebration of the liturgy of the Eucharist, Jesus actually becomes present in a very special way, especially in the bread and wine. It is not just a symbol. In this instance, the Catholic belief is quite different from that of many other Christian faiths, which consider this merely a symbolic meal.
- When the bread and wine are changed into the Body and Blood of Christ, it is the Eucharist or Holy Communion. This act is called transubstantiation. When this occurs, the physical characteristics of the bread and wine remain the same (color, texture, weight, and so on) while the substance (or its essential nature) changes.
- Almost all of the Eucharistic prayer comes from various parts of the Bible.

Communion is the ultimate sign of union with God.

- When Catholics receive Communion, the act is the ultimate sign of their union with God and one another (COmmUNION—get it?). In fact, the Eucharist is one of the three sacraments of initiation. Even though Catholics are considered members of the Church when they are baptized, they aren't considered *fully* initiated until they have made their First Communion and are then confirmed.
- When Catholics receive Holy Communion, the priest (or other minister) presents the Eucharist (also called the host) to them and says, "The Body of Christ." The person then responds, "Amen." Amen is a way of saying

"I believe" or "It is true" or "Yes!" "Amen" expresses the Catholics' belief that they are truly receiving the Body and Blood of Jesus Christ.

- Because this gesture is such an important symbol of Catholic unity, it should reflect the unity of the people involved. Receiving Communion reflects that you also truly believe in Christ's presence in the Eucharist. So if you are not Catholic, you are asked to not take Communion. You are not excluded, though. When others are receiving the Eucharist, you are invited to come up for a blessing. Just get in line with everyone else and when you get close to the front, cross your arms over your chest—this tells the priest or other minister that you wish to receive a blessing. Most non-Catholic students do this; it is not a sign of a commitment to the Catholic Church or anything like that. It just means that they are happy you are with them and that God loves and cares about you just as much. If you are not comfortable receiving a blessing, that is fine too. You can just remain seated as the others go forward.

Learn aerobics—the Catholic way.

When non-Catholics come to Mass, they often feel like they've mistakenly attended an aerobics class at the local gym. The congregation goes back and forth between sitting, standing, and kneeling. It is too complicated to explain here, but if you do not want to call attention to yourself, just stand when everyone else stands. When everyone sits, you should sit. The same goes for kneeling.

And don't worry—not even all the Catholics have it down. Quite often the priest has to remind *them* when to do things too.

 ## The Church has seasons and signs and symbols.

Catholics use different colors for different seasons in the Church year. The colors of the priests' vestments (clothing) and the church's décor vary depending on the season. The Church year doesn't really have anything to do with winter, spring, summer, or fall. Here is a list of the Church seasons and the colors that go with them:

- **Advent.** A time of preparation for Christmas, as well as the second coming of Christ; purple symbolize this time of preparation and penance.
- **Christmas.** Celebration of Christ's birth, of God's becoming a human; white is the symbolic color of this season.
- **Ordinary Time.** Called "ordinary" because the weeks are numbered (ordinal numbers); the vestments and décor are green.
- **Lent.** The forty days before Easter; again the use of purple indicates a time of preparation and penance.
- **Easter.** The celebration of Christ's victory over death; white is the symbolic color of this season.
- **On some occasions red is used.** These days are usually concerned with the Holy Spirit, such as Pentecost, or are feast days honoring martyrs.

What Is Up with These Retreats?

And the Spirit immediately drove [Jesus] out into the wilderness. He was in the wilderness for forty days. (Mark 1:12–13)

And after [Jesus] had dismissed the crowds, he went up the mountain by himself to pray. (Matthew 14:23)

[Jesus] would withdraw to deserted places and pray. (Luke 5:16)

Situation

One day during your theology class, the campus minister visits to tell your class about the ninth-grade retreat scheduled for the next week. He gives you a permission slip that your parents are supposed to sign. The signed permission slip allows you to leave the school campus for this event. A few students ask questions of the campus minister. Not wanting to look foolish, you keep quiet, although you have questions of your own—not a good move, by the way. Through your classmates' questions, you learn the location (the diocesan retreat center—duh!), the mode of transportation (big, yellow bus), the type of cuisine provided for lunch (pizza), and the theme of the retreat (reconciliation). But you still have no idea what a retreat is supposed to do or be or . . . even what it is.

On the top of the permission slip, in bold letters, are the words *Ninth-Grade Retreat.* "Hmm. What does this mean?" you think. Your mind returns to the first week of school—Fish Week—when the seniors initiated you into high school with various activities. You figure that this must be the second part, and it is so bad that you and your fellow ninth graders will need to make a quick get-away, hence the word *retreat.* (Wrong!)

Then you remember that your fellow classmates showed considerable interest in and excitement about this endeavor. You figure that a retreat is probably some kind of religious thing because it was announced in theology class. You begin to relax again, but you still do not know what actually is going to take place. You are completely clueless.

How to Handle the Situation

The handy editors and writers of the *9th Grade Survival Guide* are proud to provide you with this solid and succinct definition of the word *retreat:*

> **retreat** (ri-'trēt) *n* **1** a quick escape **2** moving away to regroup and formulate a new tactic **3** a time to get to know yourself, others, and God better

So then, which is it? An escape, a regrouping, or a time to get to know God? The answer is yes! It is all of these. In military terms, a retreat is called for when the battle is at a dead end, and it is best to quickly exit the scene to design a new strategy or plan of attack.

In spiritual terms, a retreat can be taken alone or with a group. Either way, it is a time to get away from the normal flow of life to prayerfully find out what God's plan for you is. Stepping back and examining where you have been and where you should be going is good practice. Lest you think you are beyond such an endeavor, read the Bible to see how often Jesus took time out to retreat from the active life to speak and listen to God. If Jesus did this, would not it be all the more necessary for you—for all of us?

So what can you expect to do on a retreat? The answer is difficult because retreats vary in so many ways. There are individual and group retreats, indoor and outdoor retreats, silent retreats, family retreats, writing retreats, meditative retreats, retreats in which you are physically active. The list could go on for pages. Nonetheless, retreats at Catholic schools tend to fall into a few categories, which will be explained in succeeding paragraphs. Remember that a particular school might offer a completely different experience than the ones described here and that this list is inadequate. But you will find a rousing roll of retreats that reasonably could be rendered at your high school—and some tips for having a wonderful retreat experience.

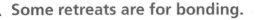 Some retreats are for bonding.

A Catholic school is first and foremost a Christian community—a Church. Bonding retreats focus on establishing some unity among the members of a particular community, be it your entire grade level or just a small class. This kind of retreat offers time for people to get to know one another and to build trust among the members of the group. This retreat is especially beneficial when the members of a group (such as ninth graders) do not know one another very well.

 Service and mission retreats are about service to others.

One of the main goals of Catholic education is to encourage students to become men and women of service. Service and mission retreats consist of active experiences in which members serve their brothers and sisters in need and then reflect on those experiences in terms of deciding how to live as Christian servants. In some cases, the experience might consist of serving meals to those who are homeless at a local soup kitchen. Some people might devote longer periods of time, such as their spring break, to traveling to another country to examine how they can fulfill their responsibilities as Christians to those beyond their country's borders. However this kind of experience is fulfilled, it is an active engagement combined with reflection.

Discovering yourself retreats are about you.

This kind of retreat attempts to give people the opportunity and the comfort to discover and reveal who they truly are behind their masks. These retreats offer a time for retreat-goers to discard that camouflage and to affirm one another as who they truly are—people made in the image and likeness of God.

 A life in Christ retreat looks at Jesus's life.

This kind of retreat sometimes addresses the questions Jesus posed to his disciples—questions such as "Who do you say that I am?" (Matthew 16:15). This kind of retreat is devoted to examining the life of Jesus Christ and exploring how your lifestyle adheres to his example.

 A kairos retreat is a favorite.

The kairos retreat is a three-day experience that aims to give the participants a deeper love for God, themselves, and one another. *Kairos* is a Greek term denoting quality or meaningful time as opposed to strictly linear time. Revealing too much about a retreat can spoil the event (see "Participate, don't anticipate" in the succeeding paragraphs). It is safe to say that this is a favorite retreat among many high school students.

Seniors look back and forward at a sending forth retreat.

Appropriate especially for exiting seniors, this retreat offers students a chance to look back on their lives as well as forward. It focuses on how the participants plan to live out their Christian journey.

Here's what you should know about attending retreats.

- **Be sure to obtain a list of items that you should bring with you.** There is nothing worse than taking a shower and realizing that you do not have a towel.
- **Relax and enjoy yourself.** Most retreats are extremely enjoyable, even during the "serious" parts.
- **Be honest.** The only part you need to play is your own.
- **Participate, don't anticipate.** Like a good mystery novel, retreats can be spoiled if you know the ending. No, someone will not jump out to scare you. Many times, retreats are simply arranged in a way that takes the retreatants through a process. Putting the last part first is like baking a cake before all the ingredients have been added—it just does not work right.
- **Know and respect your comfort zone.** Do not feel like you have to reveal or do something you are really not comfortable with.
- **Take a chance.** Although you need to respect your comfort zone, taking some chances is also important.

During the retreat, reveal a small detail about yourself that you have not told anyone before.

- **The retreat will be whatever you make it.** The retreat leaders can only plan a good retreat. They cannot make it happen. That is up to you and the rest of the participants. You need to actively do your part for it to be a great experience.

- **Pray! Speak to God and do not forget to listen to God.** Listen to God speak through your thoughts. Listen to God speak to you through the voices of your companions. Listen to God in the silence. Listen to God through the Mass. Listen to God through the Bible. Listen, listen, listen.

The fear of the LORD is the beginning of knowledge;
fools despise wisdom and instruction.

(Proverbs 1:7)

Situation

Your theology class is about to begin on the first day of school. Biology, math, and English classes were pretty much what you expected. There were no real differences between these classes and what you experienced at your previous school. You are feeling pretty confident so far.

But theology class will be different. This is your first year in a Catholic school and you just know that everyone else in your class has been in Catholic school since kindergarten. They will know all the answers, and you will be miles behind them. You'll end up with a bad grade. Your anxiety builds. Your stomach does a few somersaults. The last thing you want to do is stick out like a sore thumb on your first day of school.

You sit down in the classroom; everything is fine so far. The class begins with a prayer. Oh, no, the Hail Mary. Until today, the only thing the Hail Mary had meant to you was that it was a last-ditch football pass. You put your head down in an attempt to look prayerful, mumbling some barely audible noises in the vain hope that you look like you know what you're doing. After the prayer, you raise your head, sure that everyone sees the "non-Catholic" stamp on your forehead.

"What are we going to do in this class?" you ask yourself. "Do Catholics read the Bible? Do they always have to do what the priest says?" The questions keep coming.

How to Handle the Situation

Catholic schools place as much, if not more, importance on the spiritual life of their students as they do on other areas. That is why every semester you will have a theology class devoted to an aspect of Catholic faith life. These classes usually include study of the Scriptures, Church history, morality, sacraments, Christian social justice, and a number of interesting electives.

Not much can help prepare you for theology class, but a little coaching can clear the confusion concerning this conspicuously Catholic class.

 You'll discover the Catholic way of reading and understanding the Bible.

- Catholics do not read the Bible literally. Instead, they approach the Bible by considering the literary form, the historical circumstances, the author, and the audience. You will study the entire Bible before you begin the classes that try to make some sense out of any part of it. It sounds like a lot of work and sometimes it is, but the hard work pays off with a rich and full understanding of God's message.

- The Catholic Church teaches that faith and truth cannot be in conflict. Catholics also believe that some things in the Bible are symbolic and not meant to be taken literally. So when, for instance, the Bible says that some human beings lived to be over 900 years old, it is not necessarily meant to be taken as historical fact.

- The Catholic Bible has seven more books than the versions used by other faiths. Called the Deuterocanonical (or "second canon") books, Tobit, Judith, 1 and 2 Maccabees, Wisdom, Sirach, and Baruch are all found in the Old Testament. These books are sometimes listed in other Christian bibles under the name Apocrypha (meaning "hidden").

 ## You'll explore basic Catholic theology.

- Theology class addresses and even tests your faith, but you will not be tested on your faith. Generally the tests attempt to measure your understanding of a particular element of the Catholic faith, not your belief in it. In other words, when you take a test, you should feel comfortable in your responses because you are being asked what the Catholic Church's stance is, not what your belief is.

- Try not to worry about how different the Catholic Church is from other Christian faiths. The different faiths have far more in common than they have differences.
- It is important to know that the Catholic Church has great respect for all the world's major religions. The followers of the different Christian religions have the same ancestors in faith as their Jewish and Muslim brothers and sisters. "The Catholic Church rejects nothing that is true and holy in these religions. She regards with sincere reverence those ways of conduct and of life, those precepts and teachings which . . . often reflect a ray of that Truth which enlightens all men" (*Nostra Aetate,* number 2).

 ## This is what is covered in theology class.

Theology classes vary from school to school. For instance, some larger schools have the ability to offer a number of different electives, while smaller schools with their smaller staffs do not have that flexibility. Nonetheless, the following list offers an overview of the classes you are likely to take.

- **Catholicism.** This class provides an overview of the Catholic faith.
- **Christology.** This class is a study of Jesus of Nazareth, who has been given the title of Christ.
- **The Scriptures.** You will probably have at least a half, and usually a full, year of classes devoted to studying the Old and New Testaments of the Bible.

- **Church History.** Usually one semester is devoted to studying the Catholic Church's unique and interesting road to the present day.
- **Sacraments.** The sacraments are an essential element of Catholic life. This class usually is the most interesting (and admittedly, sometimes the most confusing) for non-Catholics.
- **Social Justice.** This class examines how everyone can respond to the common call of all Christians "to do justice, and to love kindness, and to walk humbly with your God" (Micah 6:8).
- **Morality.** The values of the Gospels help Christians decide what is good and evil, but such decisions are not so easy when the Gospels never mention issues such as nuclear war, stem cell research, pollution, and other modern dilemmas.
- **Electives.** Depending on your school, you might have some options for your senior-year theology class. Electives might include topics such as medical ethics, apologetics, racism, world religions, death and dying, spirituality, parenting, the Holocaust, and other interesting issues.

⚠️ Here are some other details unique to Catholicism.

- Saints are those who have lived an exemplary Christian life and who Catholics believe are now united with God in heaven. Catholics do not pray to saints, but they do ask the saints to pray for them. Because Christians believe in life after death, they believe that their brothers and sisters who have died have really just gone to the life after this one. In the same way that they ask other Christians here on Earth to pray for them, Catholics ask the saints to pray for them too. Canonized saints are those who are recognized by the Church and to whom all people can appeal. But there are certainly many more people in God's heavenly presence. These people can also be addressed in prayer by those who knew them well. For example, in prayer, you might ask a loved one who has passed away to intercede with God on your behalf.

- Mary holds a special place in the life of Catholics because of her role as the Mother of God. Catholics consider Mary to be the highest among all the saints. She is honored with several feast days throughout the year, including the Immaculate Conception, which celebrates her being conceived without original sin.

NOTES

Part IV
Dilemmas to Deal With

How could she say that? What should I say to her? That's just not fair! What should I wear? Who cares what he thinks?! I hate it when . . . What do you think I should do?

High school, like the rest of life, will have its share of difficult times. You will have tough choices to make and situations that will try your patience and sanity. You can't escape them, but despite what your emotions might tell you, you do not want to escape them. These situations are like the fertilizer a gardener uses. Dragging heavy plastic bags of fertilizer around is hard work, and the smell is awful, but in the end the gardener has a well nourished and beautiful garden.

Another helpful way to look at the difficult times is to use a sports analogy. Preparing for a competition is grueling. You might have to lift weights or run until your body is exhausted and your muscles ache. The muscles hurt because they tear, ever so minutely, when you put them under that kind of stress, but the healing of those small tears is what causes the muscles to grow. The repeated practices prepare you for the game.

The dilemmas you will face in high school do the same. They are smelly and difficult to lug around. They are painful and sometimes exhaust your energy. Yet, hopefully, after you have survived each one, you will have a beautiful and strong result. You will be better prepared for the next part of life, which will be without as many support systems (your parents, friends, family, and so on) around all the time.

But do not make the mistake of thinking that high school is just practice for real life. No, it is *all* real life. The friendships you make, the joy and the pain you feel, are all real. High school is just a step into the deeper side of the swimming pool (minus the flippers and the water wings).

What follows are a few myths about the joys and the pains of high school and the reasons why they are myths.

The Best Four Years Myth

Think about it. If high school is the best four years of your life, then it must be all downhill after your senior year. I hope this is not true for you (especially if high school is not that great an experience for you). After high school is the rest of life and so much to experience that can be genuinely fulfilling: college, career, marriage, parenthood, religious life, friendships, service to others, music and art, travel. It is good to hope that high school will be great, but it might be better to look at it as the next step in the great adventure.

The Most Wretched Four Years Myth

High school is a time of change and growth, but you can count on some good times as well. High school will have numerous opportunities for fun and laughter. Many people make their best friends for life in high school. On another level, these years are also an opportune time to take a deeper look into your blossoming spiritual life.

The Facing Dilemmas Alone Myth

Although it is true that you will be called on to be more responsible for your work and behavior, you will not be left alone to sink to the bottom of the pool. In fact, the situation is no different from when you were younger. When you were five years old, your parents probably made you hold their hands when you crossed the street. Not long after that, they let you cross the street alone under their supervision. Later, you were allowed to do it alone. Similarly, as you go through high school, you will be given more and more responsibilities and duties. But it doesn't happen all at once. Nonetheless, your ninth-grade year is a big step and you should prepare for it. Your teachers and parents will not let you drown, but they might let you flail your arms a bit before help arrives. After a while, though, if you go under and do not come back up, most likely it will be because you chose not to swim, not because help was not available. Your teachers, counselors, and parents will be there for you.

What You Will Find in This Section

Everyone faces dilemmas in high school. You cannot avoid them, but you can handle them in better or worse ways. That is why the following chapters are in your hands:

- Drama! Rumors, Gossip, and Such
- Finding Your Right Fit
- Balancing School, Family, Friends, and Fun
- Finding True Friends
- Dealing with Disappointment

Navigating the drama, rumors, and gossip in
high school can be a challenge.

Drama! Rumors, Gossip, and Such

"I tell you, on the day of judgment you will have to give an account for every careless word you utter." (Matthew 12:36)

"The truth will make you free." (John 8:32)

Situation

On a Saturday afternoon like any other in Ashley's first semester of high school, she logged on to her computer. She had decided early in the semester to make a rule that she would finish her homework on Saturday morning so that she could enjoy the rest of the weekend without any worries. Now finished with her assignments, she went to the Web site where students congregate online. In this virtual school community, students vented about school, shared music, talked about teachers, and of course, gossiped. In fact, this Web site was where she had found out that Jacob, her now-boyfriend, had broken up with his ex-girlfriend. In Ashley's mind, this was a great place to find out the latest scoop on the school's social scene. A lot happens between three o'clock Friday afternoon and seven o'clock Monday morning, and Ashley did not want to be out of the loop.

After chatting with her best friend on the instant-message page, Ashley clicked over to the chat room where students from all over her school posted the latest goings-on. She noticed that a new person was online—"Jani15." Ashley discovered that Jani15 was Janice, one of her best friends. Janice had never been to this Web site before because her parents did not allow it and had blocked the site on her computer. Ashley learned that Janice talked her parents into letting her get on as long as they were in the same room. And this was not all that Ashley found out.

After a few minutes of gossip, Janice warned Ashley that she was going to tell her something pretty painful. Ashley braced herself. Then, Janice told her that she had seen Ashley's boyfriend, Jacob, on a date at the movie theater with someone else the night before. Ashley could not believe the words she saw on the screen. Janice told her everything she had seen, including the name of the girl he was with—Christina.

Ashley immediately logged off the computer and began to cry. She felt sick to her stomach. She was hurt and angry. Without thinking, she got online again and went right to Christina's Web site, where she wrote the most horrible things she could think of. She used every insult and every foul word available to her. She vented all her anger as she banged on the keyboard. Now not only would this girl know how Ashley felt, but the whole school would see what kind of person she was for stealing her boyfriend.

With that accomplished, she turned her attention to her boyfriend. She decided to not let him off the hook so easily. She decided to call him on the phone and catch him in his lie. She dialed his phone number and he answered.

"Hi, Jacob! How's it going?" Her cheery tones were faked perfectly.

"Great! How are things with you?" Jacob replied.

After the conversation journeyed through the opening niceties, Ashley made her move. Jacob had told her that he was going to stay home Friday night to work on his history paper. She decided to ask him about it. "So Jacob, how is your paper coming? Are you finished?"

"No, not yet. I still have some more to write."

"Wow," Ashley remarked. "You sure had a lot of time to get it done. You must have not focused very hard. Maybe you should not have taken that break at the movie theater!" Ashley was ready for Jacob to try to squirm out of that one.

"What? I wasn't at the movies last night. I was at home."

"No, you weren't," Ashley cried. "You were at the movie theater with Christina. You are lying to me! How could you do this to me?"

Jacob rebutted, "No, I wasn't at the movie theater with Christina. I was at home writing my paper. Who told you this?"

"Janice just told me fifteen minutes ago. She was online at that Web site, and she told me that she saw you last night at the movie theater."

Jacob was silent for a moment. He then slowly said, "Ashley, listen. Janice is not allowed on that Web site. Her parents won't let her go on."

Ashley interrupted, "Yes, but now she can. Her parents let her if they are in the same room and can watch what's going on."

"Ashley, let me finish. Fifteen minutes ago Janice could not have told you that she saw me at the movies last night. First of all, I was not at the movies. Second of all, Janice has been at the movies with my sister for the past hour."

Ashley was confused. She sat in stunned silence. Her mind raced backward in time. She remembered all those horrible things she had said to Jacob. She recalled all the awful comments she had left on Christina's Web page. She went back to the conversation she had online with Janice. Oh no! It wasn't really Janice.

How to Handle the Situation

Without a doubt, you will hear a lot of gossip in high school. Sooner or later, one of the rumors will be about you or one of your friends. How you react can sometimes make or break a friendship, and it is important to handle these situations with care.

⚠ Go to the source.

- When betting on horse races, gamblers say that their best information comes from the innermost circles of the horse-racing community. The joke is that the best information comes from the one who really knows how the race will go—the horse. If you hear something that is actually worth checking out, go directly to the person it concerns and get it "straight from the horse's mouth."

- Stay honest. If you have been a continually honest person, hopefully your friends will feel comfortable enough to get it from "the horse's mouth" when they hear rumors about you.

 ## Give me just the facts, ma'am.

- The 1950s television show *Dragnet* was about a detective who investigated various crimes. In his search for the truth, he became famous for getting people to stick to "the facts." This is good advice when it comes to dealing with the school rumor mill as well.
- If the rumors are important enough to investigate (which should be rare), then focus on people who have firsthand knowledge and try to get them to stick to the facts, not their opinions.

 ## Even if true, gossip is still not okay.

- Truthful information will often become twisted after it has been passed around by word of mouth. Did you ever play the "Telephone Game" when you were a kid? In the game, one person whispers something to another and the message is relayed through numerous people. Finally, the last person says the whisper out loud and, almost always, it is very different from what the first person said.

- Even when the information is true, gossip often concerns private information. Everyone has a right to privacy and should not have to bear the constant scrutiny of their classmates.

 If you are just listening, you are still participating.

- Just because you do not spread the rumors does not mean that you are innocent. When you listen to gossip, you give it attention and therefore acknowledge the teller as doing something important. This is all the encouragement he or she needs to continue doing more.

Stop gossip in its tracks.

- Imagine how you would feel if someone were to spread rumors about you and your friends listened to the rumors and did not speak up. Do not just sit there and let it happen. Speak up!
- When you hear gossip on the loose, stop it right away by simply refusing to participate in gossiping about someone or by questioning the authenticity of the gossip.

Ignoring it is sometimes the best policy.

- When you deny gossip and it still does not die, sometimes it's best to just ignore it. Sooner or later people will get bored with it or another rumor will get their attention.
- Have confidence in yourself. Have confidence in the truth. Keep faith in the fact that the "truth will make you free" (John 8:32).

Finding Your Right Fit

It was he who created humankind in the beginning, and he left them in the power of their own free choice.

(Sirach 15:14)

Situation

Two months of your ninth-grade year have passed and your mother has been on your case about getting out to meet some new people. You are not the most outgoing person, but secretly you do see your mother's point. Just to avoid another night of nagging, in the presence of your mother, you grab the school handbook and open it to the section that covers school clubs. You smack your hand down on the first club your finger finds and say to your mom, "Okay, Mom, enough! I am going to go to the . . . uh . . ." You quickly dart your eyes to find the club's name just above your fingertip in the book. ". . . the . . . uh . . . Culinary Club. Yes, the Culinary Club! Are you satisfied, Mom?" She walks away with a curious smile on her face. "Hmm, what is she thinking?"

Ah. Relief. You now can breathe easily. And hey, you were secretly interested in getting out of the house a little more often anyway. But a question haunts you: what does one do in the Culinary Club? Perhaps one culinates? You pick up the dictionary and look up the word *culinate* to find no such entry. You think, "Maybe it is something like archery or fencing? Aaah, I'll just take a chance."

The next day you check in with Mr. Ondak, the club's moderator, to find out when and where the next meeting will be. He tells you that the first gathering will be this Friday and looks through the several large piles of paper on his messy desk to find the time and the place, as well as a list of ingredients for you to bring. "Ingredients?" you ask. You are shocked to learn that *culinary* has something to do with cooking.

Oh, no. You hate cooking. Even the challenge of making a peanut butter and jelly sandwich turns your stomach. Just last week you had to pull out the recipe book to make toast. And once, when you were nine years old, your mother made you help her cook dinner and . . . let's just say that by the end of the evening, rice decorated the walls, your dog was covered in tomato sauce, and your father ordered in Chinese food. At this point in your life, you vaguely remember the incident but have dismissed it as youthful inexperience. This time things will be different. You are confident that you can master this cooking thing.

Nonetheless, you thank Mr. Ondak as he hands you a list of club members. "Here it is!" he says as he hands it to you. "It'll be my first meeting too. I'm the new moderator." You do not know one person on that list.

Friday night arrives and you show up with your share of the ingredients for a recipe that sounds exotic: *suppli alla telefono.* You will soon learn that this is Italian stuffed rice balls. You are just in time to meet the student's parents who are leaving for the night and putting the house in the care of Mr. Ondak. As luck would have it, the first meeting for the Culinary Club also falls on the night of your first high school date, but the timing is perfect. You will leave the club meeting at seven-thirty, just in time to meet your date at the movie theater at eight. Besides, you told your mom you were going to get involved and you definitely don't want to have a conversation about your missing the first meeting.

The evening begins with Mr. Ondak briefly explaining the menu. Your confidence begins to grow—you can do this. Mr. Ondak continues talking about the way the rice will be prepared. Okay, that sounds a little complicated, but you are prepared. You quickly speak up, "I'll be in charge of stirring the sauce, if that's okay with everyone." The group nods their agreement, a little taken aback by your sudden burst of enthusiasm. The evening progresses nicely. There you stand, in front of the stove, wooden spoon in hand before a pot of tomato sauce. As you chat it up with your new friends, you realize that the directions said to simmer over low heat and you have the stove cranked all the way up. Hoping no one catches your mistake, you quickly turn the heat down and pry the lid from the pot. Almost in slow motion you see the sauce spurt out of the pot in a rolling boil all over the front of your shirt. As you scream in horror, one of your new friends takes the sound to mean you are in pain and throws his cup of cola on you to cool you down. In all the commotion, the pot of sauce spills on your pants legs and new shoes. There you stand in a puddle of the ruined meal, dripping with cola and sauce. You have ten minutes to meet your date. You are still hungry, and you wish that you had thought a little more about your choice of extracurricular activity.

How to Handle the Situation

Finding the best extracurricular activity for you is going to be part science, part personality, and part luck. We cannot help you with your luck, but we can help you with ways to whittle down the numerous possibilities before you.

What sounds interesting?

- Look at all the clubs the school has to offer. What sounds interesting? exotic? fun? helpful? adventurous? Answering this simple question will give you the main criteria for deciding which club to join.
- Popular does not always mean better. Just because seventy-five ninth graders go paintballing once a month does not mean that you will like it too. Focus on the activity itself. If it is something you think you will really enjoy, then it will probably be a better fit for you, regardless of how many people go. And a small group might allow you more power when it comes time to make important decisions for the club. Sometimes people can get lost or feel left out in large groups.
- Maybe you have a hobby that would be great for a club, but you cannot find anything like it on the school's list. What do you do then? Start your own. Most of the time, the only thing that a club needs to become a sponsored school organization is a moderator and approval from the administration. If you have something that you think will work, ask a teacher who you think would

make a good moderator for that group for help and advice.

Do your research.

- Learn about the moderator—usually a teacher but sometimes another member of the school staff or administration. Does this person really know about the activities involved? Some moderators inherit a club in which they are not really interested. The previous moderator, who was great, might have left the school and a new teacher was asked to take over. Even though the new moderator works hard to make it fun, sometimes the activity is just not their thing.
- Find out who the members are and ask them about the club. Do they have fun? What do they do when they meet?

Make sure you have the time and the resources.

- How often does the group meet? for how long? Can you handle the extra time away from your family and your studies? Will the group's activities conflict with major family events such as reunions or trips?
- Are there any club dues to pay? Do you have to buy a uniform or a club T-shirt? Can you afford the activities?
- Before you join a club, discuss it with your parents. Because the club will take a considerable amount of your time, and your parents will probably be the ones

paying for your club activities, you will want them to be part of the decision.

Don't judge a book by its cover.

- At first glance, the Rocketry Team might sound like a bunch of geeks who get together to talk about space ships. But did you know that the members of this group actually build rockets and compete against other schools? They travel all over the country for national competitions whose judges are from little groups such as . . . uh . . . NASA! Students can win scholarships and prizes. It is no small thing.
- A group's popularity does not always mean that it is the best one for you, but sometimes a group popular because it is a lot of fun. Keep your ear to ground and listen for the campus favorites.

Think of fun and service.

- One of the essential elements of Catholic schools is service. This element also exists with clubs. You will find clubs that serve those who are poor, that work for right-to-life issues, that help increase environmental awareness, that encourage political awareness, that help end racism and prejudice, and that focus their activities on the needs of the their neighbors.
- Make sure you balance your involvement and include service clubs in your life. A self-centered life is no life at all.

Don't make balancing your life a high-wire act.

Balancing School, Family, Friends, and Fun

Honest balances and scales are the LORD's;
all the weights in the bag are his work.

(Proverbs 16:11)

"For what will it profit them to gain the whole world and forfeit their life?" (Mark 8:36)

Situation

Your first semester is at an end and high school has been going great. You made the honor roll; your cross-country track team made it to the state finals where you came in second place in your division; your bid for the student council was victorious; you successfully convinced school administrators and your fellow council members to move the ninth- and tenth-grade Valentine dance from the gymnasium to a nice, reasonably priced location; you started driver's education classes; and you are considering contributing some of your writings to a high school textbook company that is looking for material from young writers. You just cannot imagine a better start to your high school career.

At home, your parents have been supportive. They are encouraged by your fantastic attitude and your determination to succeed. They brag to their friends about your consistent work ethic and post your report cards on the refrigerator for your younger siblings to see. They ooze with pride.

Or they did. Lately, they do not seem as happy. You write it off to trouble with one of your younger brothers or sisters, or maybe they are having an annoying parental mood swing. Your friends seem to have a bit of attitude as well. Jealousy! Yes, they be jealous because you are doing so well.

One day you come home for dinner. "Nice to see you," your dad scornfully remarks. You think, "Why the rude comment?" as you wipe off the dust from your chair at the dinner table. Your mother exclaims to your three-year-old sister, "Look who's here! I think (fill-in-your-name-here) needs a BIG HUG!" Your little sister runs right past you to the living room and comes back tightly clutching your eighth-grade portrait. The poor darling now considers her oldest sibling to be a wooden picture frame with your inserted photo, rather than the human form next to her at the dinner table. One could say that you finally "get the picture."

You tell your family that you are going to spend a little more time at home. Your dad assists you by adding "and church" to your sentence. You mutter, "Oh yeah," as you remember staying up so late working on a student council project Saturday night that you were too tired to go to Mass with the family the next morning. Then you remember that you also had a history class essay due on Monday and spent the rest of your waking hours researching and writing. By the time you looked up at the clock, the last church service of the day had come and gone.

You realize the error of your ways, and your parents understand as you promise to do better. You decide that your friends will also get a little more of your attention, so you call a friend to ask her to join your family for a barbecue dinner next Saturday (why not kill two birds with one stone, huh?). Your friend sounds a little distant and politely declines. She tells you that she already has plans with Steven. "Steven?" you say. "I thought you hated Steven!"

"No, we've been friends for a while now. We got to know each other when we were forced to do that project on Icelandic horses."

"Oh yeah," you say, trying to sound like you remember what she's talking about. "That Icelandic horse thing. Yeah, that's when you guys seemed to get over that hate thing. Icelandic horses will do that. They have that emotional healing kind of vibe going for them."

"Okay. Uh . . . well, I have to go now. I . . . uh . . . need to brush my dog's hair." Click.

Hmmm, you realize that you have done it. Not only have you ignored your parents, your siblings, and your spiritual life, but you have ignored your friends too. And they do not seem to be as understanding as your family. They seem to have moved on, probably because you seem to have done the same.

How to Handle the Situation

You may be handling the balance within school, but that doesn't mean you are handling the balance within your life. In their desire to help ninth graders start off on a good note at high school, many adults forget to emphasize that one important element for maintaining sanity is understanding that school is not everything.

As Jesus noted to his disciples, one must deny self and one's desires to be there for others. Otherwise, you can end up with all the awards and honors, and have no one with whom to share them. In a self-centered haze, a person can also lose sight of God. But there are ways to help you avoid this downward self-indulgent spiral. Read on.

Keep a calendar.

- Keeping a calendar regularly can help resolve many of these issues. In a flawed attempt to keep spontaneity in their lives, some people avoid calendars, but if an event is important enough to do, it is important enough to schedule.
- Be sure to keep all kinds of events in your calendar— not just school events. If you look in it to plan a day to work on a project with a friend and you do not have your family camping trip marked in, you will soon find yourself among some pretty angry people.

Learn to say no.

- Saying no is difficult for some people. In an effort to avoid hurting or angering friends or family members, you might be tempted to say yes to everyone and sort it out later. Resist that temptation because you will only end up with chaos and make everyone upset in the end.

- A good policy is to be honest and consistent. When you cannot attend an event because you are booked, say something like, "No, I can't. I would really like to do this, but I am already booked that day." Though initially such an approach might be a little harder, people will have more respect and consideration for your efforts and honesty.
- Offer an alternative time if it is something you really want to do.
- Do not feel obligated to tell people why you are saying no. They do not have a right to know what you have going on in your life. Feel free to be vague or offer a humorous response.
- If you really do not want to do something, politely say, "No, thank you," and move on. If you keep putting off the inevitable, you will only annoy the person who invited you and make an uncomfortable situation last much longer than it should.

⚠ Communicate with parents and teachers.

- Your parents will handle things much better if you let them know ahead of time that you will be gone for an event. Telling them at the last minute will only increase the household stress level. Good communication also helps eliminate the last-minute "No, you can't go tonight and here is why" speech that is destined to happen on the night of the most important event of your life.

- Parents, teachers, and friends can also offer alternatives to situations that you haven't thought of. Talk to them. Two brains are better than one.

⚠️ Prioritize but maintain flexibility.

- Sometimes your family will be the most important recipient of your time and attention, but final exam week will probably not be one of those times.
- Life happens. Illness strikes. People die. Tragedy befalls you. When this happens, there are more important things than school and extracurricular activities that need your attention. Do not give up easily, but realize that sometimes the best thing is to let go of one of your goals.
- It is not always about you. Sometimes you have to let go of your own wants to take care of others: spending time with a younger sibling who looks up to you, doing chores, helping your dad around the house when your mom is away on a business trip, or helping with your church youth group's service project to feed the poor in your city.

Finding True Friends

Faithful friends are a sturdy shelter:
>whoever finds one has found a treasure.

>(Sirach 6:14)

You will know them by their fruits. (Matthew 7:16)

"Judas, is it with a kiss that you are betraying the Son of Man?" (Luke 22:48)

Situation Number 1

Suppose you are a student who has just moved into the area and does not know a single soul at the new school (even if this is not true for you, just pretend that it is). The friends at your junior high were the best. They were there for you in good times and in bad. They were the kind of friends who could finish your sentences. They were the friends you invited to your third-grade birthday party where that new kid split open his pants, revealing his Spiderman underwear. (No wonder he left your school that year—he probably never recovered from that experience.)

These were the pals who laughed whenever you said the words *orange juice.* The sight of you and your friends giggling their heads off drew stares from others nearby because, of course, they did not know about the "Clarence Incident" in the lunchroom back in fifth grade

. . . the time when Clarence started laughing while he was drinking orange juice. But now at the new high school, they are not there. In fact, during the first week of school, you could not help but laugh a little every time the cafeteria lady offered you some orange juice. The students behind you in line started to think that you were a little "off."

Those old friends are irreplaceable. No, those friends only come once in a lifetime, and now they are back at home . . . well, your *old* home. Your new school does not feel much like home. The question haunting you is, Will it ever feel like home?

Situation Number 2

You are in the beginning of the second semester and have been working hard to make a good start in your new school. You have successfully balanced your academic and social lives by nurturing each one with a sufficient amount of time and attention, enabling both to flourish. You are also a noteworthy athlete who has received the respect of the coaches and the rest of the school staff. Everything is coming up roses. You cannot imagine a better start.

And what about all the new friends you have made? You have one new friend with whom you have become quite close. This friend is different from the others because you seem to be kind of a mentor to this person. He has not been as successful as you, and he often speaks highly of your academic achievements as well as your successes in sports. He is a lot of fun too, so you enjoy helping him out from time to time with his homework.

Then, a few weeks into the second semester, your world comes crashing down. You are called into the office of the dean (the school administrator who handles disciplinary problems). In the dean's office, you see your recent world history essay paper on his desk and your new friend in the chair next to the one the dean asks you to sit in.

You cannot imagine what's happening, but the dean spells it out for you. You are being accused of cheating on your history essay with your new friend, who has already confessed to it. Your buddy admitted to writing the first half of the essay and claimed that you completed the second half. Bewildered, you deny this and ask your friend why he is lying. You took the time to help him write his paper and this is how he repays you?

Then you recall the moment when he must have taken your paper. He was at your house after school one day and said that he was having difficulty writing his essay. You pulled up your paper on the computer to show him how to write a proper heading and then explained what the teacher would look for and other details. You remember taking a quick break to go to the bathroom. He must have printed it out then.

You feel sick to your stomach. Not only are you being accused of cheating but your friend has turned on you. You sink into the chair in the dean's office trying to figure a way out of this dilemma, but all you can think about are the questions: How did I get into this friendship? How could I have not seen this coming? Who is this "friend"?

How to Handle the Situation

Finding true friends is not as easy as it sounds. In fact, it is almost impossible to tell whether friends are "real" until you have spent a lot of time with them. Nonetheless, you can take some steps and look for certain qualities to find out whether your new buddy is the diamond in the rough or just another fair-weather friend.

"You will know them by their fruits" (Matthew 7:16).

- Most people act consistently, regardless of who is around them. If your friends gossip *to* you, they gossip *about* you. If your friends tell you that they lied to someone else, they probably feel fine lying to you. Do not think that you are going to be the exception.
- Is your friend . . . honest? trustworthy? sincere? loyal? straightforward? considerate? These are qualities that all friends should have. What other qualities do you want in a friend? Ask yourself whether you can see these qualities in your new friend.

Try the more-the-merrier approach.

- Do not get caught up in one-on-one relationships, be they romantic or otherwise. High school is a time of great changes, making these years great for exploring and meeting different kinds of people.

- Group activities take the stress out of high-pressure happenings such as the homecoming dance and the prom. Going out as a group also makes these events a lot more fun.

Look beyond the obvious.

- The people in the popular cliques are not always there because they are so nice that everyone wants to be around them. The opposite can be true as well—just because someone is not popular does not mean that person is an unlovable dweeb.
- Sometimes, opposites attract. Sometimes, a new friend is the last person you would ever have considered. Sometimes, the friendship is an obvious match. Sometimes, the friendship seems an impossible match. Be open. You do not know until you know.

Cliques are kid stuff.

- If you were to look at life in junior high, high school, and then college, you would notice that the higher the grade level, the less people feel confined by cliques. The further they go in life, the more comfortable they are with moving in and out of different groups of people. There is a lesson about maturity here. Do not wait to learn it.
- Cliques are so junior high. Just drop the clique lifestyle . . . even if some in high school have not given it up yet.

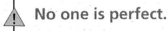# No one is perfect.

- No matter what friends you choose, they will have flaws. Everyone does. You cannot escape this fact, so you must learn to accept it if you want to have friends for longer than twenty-four hours.
- Boundaries are good. Know what behavior is unacceptable to you. You should not hang out with people who drink alcohol, do drugs, are sexually active, or participate in other dangerous activities. Know that *you are not being a friend when you overlook these kinds of behaviors.* Good friends do not silently stand by to watch their friends slowly destroy themselves.
- Forgiveness is a necessity in any kind of healthy relationship. From time to time, you will need to forgive your friends when they do not act as they should. At times, you will also need to ask for forgiveness. Do not be afraid to do this. Forgiveness is the linchpin that holds good friendships together.

Dealing with Disappointment

Suffering produces endurance, and endurance produces character, and character produces hope, and hope does not disappoint us, because God's love has been poured into our hearts. (Romans 5:3–5)

Consider the generations of old and see:
> has anyone trusted in the LORD and been disappointed?

(Sirach 2:10)

Situation

You are ready to enter or have just entered high school. You possibly have been told "high school will be the best four years of your life." Maybe it was Aunt Gladys who leaned over and pinched your cheeks like you were still four and a half years old and said: "Y'knowut, high school was the best four years of my life. And y'knowut? You are going to have the *best* time . . . the best! You are going to meet your best friends for life. It's like four years of having no worries and just having fun with your friends and you'll remember it for the rest of your life."

Let us take a moment to consider on this situation. Let's first focus on the life of your sweet but particularly miserable Aunt Gladys. True, high school was the best four years of her life, but honestly—the twenty-six years since high school have been wretched for her.

To spare you the nasty details, let's just say that after failing out of junior college, life for Gladys was a steep-sloped downhill cruise. So when your Aunt Gladys says that high school was the best four years of her life, you might want to put that statement into some perspective, but do not let Gladys know. Just smile and let her have her moment.

Will high school be the best four years of your life? You'd better hope not. It's not that high school will be so bad, but you do not want your life to reach its peak at the ripe old age of eighteen. If high school is going to be the best time of your life, that means you will probably have sixty to seventy years of going downhill afterward. Please, do not wish that on yourself.

You might also hear some crusty old grouch grumbling, "Kid, wait till you get into the *real world.*" As you probably know, you already are in the "real world." Maybe he thinks you live in some alternate universe where you skip around in oblivion with a permanent smile glued to your face. Is that where you live? I did not think so.

No, where you live, friends argue, people get divorced, family members die, and workers lose their jobs—just like everywhere else. Adults tend to forget that these things affect young people too. Disappointments happen in high school just as in other times of life.

In fact, many people look back at high school with a sense of relief that they do not have to do it again. Although high school can be a fun and exciting time, it can simultaneously be difficult and painful. So much happens in the four years of high school that although four years sounds like a long time, it is a rather short period in the context of an entire life. In these four years, you will evolve from an eighth-grade graduate into someone who has learned to drive and is ready to move away from home. This requires major real-world life changes. In fact, these changes are so big that they can take you on an emotional roller coaster. The person who tells you that you are not in the real world yet needs to think again.

These words are meant not to scare you but to shine a realistic light on these four years. High school comes with both great joy and great disappointment, no different from any other time in your life, except that hopefully you will learn how to handle both with grace and gratitude. Gratitude? For disappointments? Yes. Read on.

How to Handle the Situation

No matter who you are, the chips will not always fall your way. Even though you might think that you are the only person being riddled with bad luck, do not believe it. Everyone has ups and downs—EVERYONE—no exceptions—even those who always seem to be smiling. Sooner or later something will disappoint you. You might not make the baseball team; your boyfriend or girlfriend might break up with you; you might miss making the honor roll by one point; your basketball team might lose the championship because you missed a last-second free throw; your favorite teacher might get seriously ill and have to quit; your best friend might lie to you; the class trip that you helped organize might get cancelled because of bad weather. The possibilities are endless.

The key is to remember that you cannot avoid disappointments, but you can learn to handle them well. Here are a few suggestions that should be more deserving of your attention than listening to your Aunt Gladys—not that she isn't a sweet lady, but . . .

This too will pass.

- Remember that disappointments will come and go—just like the good times. Expect them without worrying; and when they come, endure them with hope.
- When you are overwhelmed with disappointment, take time to talk to someone who has been through some tough times—a teacher or a counselor—and ask that person to share bad luck stories. These talks can be good reminders that despite difficult times, people move on and find happiness again.

Put it into perspective.

- Sometimes people get overwhelmed by disappointments. They feel like the end of the world has come when the love of their life breaks up with them. The feeling is real sadness, but the overwhelming sense of eternal loss is like a nightmare. During these times, remember that although the feeling seems eternal, sooner or later the feeling passes. Ask all the older people you know whether they have ever been dumped before. How are they now? (This works for other disappointments too.)

- When you do blow things out of proportion, do not get too down on yourself. Yes, you decided to trash the locker room after losing the baseball game where you had two players in scoring position and you blindly swung at three straight balls to record the last out of the game. Yes, it was an important game. But, in context, you did not fail to solve the world hunger problem. We all blow a gasket from time to time. Apologize, make amends, seek forgiveness, and then move on.

Learn from everything.

- Accept your disappointments. Do not avoid or ignore them, or pretend that you are not sad. Go ahead, cry and beat your pillow. In fact, that is healthy and normal. But the time does come when you need to move on. If you find yourself dwelling too much on your losses, take it as a sign to get some help.
- You can almost always find lessons in your disappointment and grief. Look for them.
- Saint Paul seemed to think that we are at our best when we are at our lowest moments. Apparently he knew that it was not good to get caught up in our successes. Rather, it is when we are needy that we find Christ. Saint Paul wrote: "I will boast all the more gladly of my weaknesses, so that the power of Christ may dwell in me. Therefore I am content with weaknesses . . . for whenever I am weak, then I am strong" (2 Corinthians 12:9–10). This is true wisdom.

NOTES

Part V
What Incoming Ninth Graders Should Know

Almost any product you buy will have instructions on how to use it. Even the most simple items have instructions. For instance, the next time you're in a store, look at a blender on the shelf. It's probably safe to say that the instructions include words like these: "Do not place fingers near the twirling sharp blades while machine is in use." Or look at a lawn mower user guide, which is likely to provide the following tidbit of wisdom: "For outdoor use only." With instructions like these everywhere, you might expect to find this sign at the high school entrance: "Warning: May contain nuts." Or this sign on a teacher's door: "May cause drowsiness."

Yet it seems that the most important things you do in life do not have any written guidelines. You might have heard your parents lamenting that none of their children came with a set of directions. The same is true for surviving a Catholic high school (at least until this book came out). What do you need to know to get through high school? Well, sure, there's algebra, biology, United States history, and all the other subjects, but what about all of the stuff in between? And how do you actually get through it all without tearing your hair out?

For example, here are some questions that might be going through your head as you prepare to begin your high school career:

- What do I do when I have too much work and I can't get it finished in time?
- What happens if I become a social outcast?
- What happens if I cheat in high school?
- What happens if I fail a class?
- What can get me kicked out of high school?

- What is the most important thing I can do to be successful?

All these are good questions, and you deserve some good honest answers to them. But some issues are not that simple—for example, how to be successful. You need to do many things to be successful, and the focus might vary from person to person. Some people might need to read every night. Others might need to review and rewrite their class notes every day. There is no simple and direct answer.

What You Will Find in This Section

This section of the book addresses a few details to keep high on your priority list as your move through high school. These details are not about how to study for tests or how to choose elective classes. It is all the stuff in between. It is the glue that holds it all together.

- Prioritize, Prioritize, Prioritize
- Don't Go It Alone
- One Mistake Is Not the End of the World
- Curing the Cooties

Prioritize, Prioritize, Prioritize

I, the LORD, am first.

(Isaiah 41:4)

Situation

You have a big history test tomorrow. You had a basketball game last night and could not study. Your parents are working late tonight and a friend, who lives around the block, has invited you to come over and watch a movie. Which of the following is the best choice to make?

    a. Blow off studying for the test and go watch the movie.

    b. Agonize over the dilemma for so long that it becomes too late to choose either one.

    c. Make a cheat sheet for the test with your friend and watch the movie.

    d. Stay home and study for the test.

If you chose a, then you need to go back and read "Balancing School, Family, Friends, and Fun." If you chose b, you might want to attend a self-help seminar on decision making. If you chose c, then take out your telephone book to find the name of the local public school you will soon be attending. If you chose d—great! Read on.

On Wednesday of next week, you have tests in English, algebra, and theology. You and other members of the student council are hosting a dance this Friday night. You have a date the next day, and you are meeting with two other students Sunday afternoon to work on a biology project that is due at the end of next week. You have regular homework assignments for the rest of your classes. Now, if a train is traveling 73 mph downhill at a 12-degree grade and the engineer is wearing a white polyester jumpsuit and screaming your biology teacher's name, when should you begin studying for that Wednesday test?

    a. I should rail against the tyrannical demands that the educational system places on me and sit in front of the television set in silent protest.

    b. Wednesday during my lunch period.

    c. It depends on whether the train engineer is left-handed or right-handed. If the engineer is a lefty, then the obvious answer is Monday at 6:47 p.m. If the engineer is right-handed, then study time commences at 9:04 p.m. Sunday (of course, this does not take into account the variances caused by the vernal equinox for the countries in the southern hemisphere).

    d. I should put down this preposterous book and start studying now.

If you chose a, then you should prepare for a career requiring the least amount of cranial activity possible. If you chose b, you should see the response to answer a. If you chose c, then perhaps a trip to the counselor's office might be beneficial (walk quickly, please). If you chose d, you answered correctly and are probably not reading this at all because you are studying—as you should be.

How to Handle the Situation

Hopefully, the above situations require simple decision-making. But the time is coming when you will not have such easy decisions to make, nor will you have a simple list of multiple-choice answers from which to select. For example, it is Tuesday afternoon and you have two tests on Wednesday. You find out that your grandmother is dangerously ill. Do you stay home to study, or do you visit your grandmother in the hospital?

Or what if you are trying to impress a prospective college with your scientific aptitude, but you have a test in your weakest subject—English—the same day as your advanced chemistry test? Do you focus on your weakest or strongest subject? Do you risk getting a D in English to ensure an A in advanced chemistry? Will the college be more upset with the low grade or more impressed with the high grade?

These are tough questions. And for tough questions, you need tough answers. For prioritizing those problematic predicaments, we're pleased to present this plentiful pile of pointers.

Ask yourself, "What is the *most important* thing to do?"

- When ranking your priorities, it is good to know where you stand on the most important things in your life.
- Someone suggested that a student's priorities should always be God, family, and then school (in that order). Another suggested that it should be family and then school, with God in every part of it. What do you think?

 These questions will help you prioritize.

- Can this be done at some other time?
- What are the effects of doing one thing and not the other? And vice versa?
- What are the pros and cons of each possibility? List them.

 Seek guidance.

- Ask your teachers for assistance when you are in a jam. They can usually offer good advice, if not fix the situation.
- Counselors can also be helpful. They can help you sift through the issues and bring up points that you should consider but might not have thought of yet. This is especially true with issues such as where to focus your attention.

- Mom and Dad are also good resources. They have been in these situations before (they probably still address situations like these all the time). Do not be shy about asking.

Ask yourself, "What would Jesus do?"

- No, you are not Jesus, and no one can assume to always know exactly what Jesus would do, but it can be a fruitful exercise in some situations.
- No, Jesus apparently did not attend high school, but he did provide principles you can use to guide your life.
- Consult the Bible. What wisdom might it have to offer on the subject?
- Pray.

NOTES

_____

_____

_____

_____

_____

_____

_____

_____

_____

_____

_____

_____

_____

_____

_____

_____

_____

_____

_____

_____

_____

Life is more rewarding when you don't go it alone.

Don't Go It Alone

Bear one another's burdens, and in this way you will fulfill the law of Christ. (Galatians 6:2)

Situation

Ninth-grade year has been going well. You have handled the first six weeks of school with the confidence and composure that would make any parent proud. But this success has come with a price—the biggest being that you have lost your normal sleep routine. With early morning football practice and the extra homework load, you have not gotten the required hours of shut-eye to keep your mind sharp. The loss of sleep is slowly taking its toll.

You have a history paper and a biology project due, and you have a test in theology—all on Monday. This is Sunday evening. Earlier this weekend, your mother had noticed your distress and offered to type your paper, but in your desire to remain self-reliant, you politely thanked your mom and refused her help. Your dad had offered to do the shopping for your project. You thanked your dad but told him that you could handle it and rode your bike to the store.

You worked on your paper and project until the wee hours of the morning both Friday and Saturday nights. Your drooping eyes betrayed your attempts to glue the pipe cleaner to the poster board. You stared blankly at your computer screen trying to figure out something to write. You concluded that both the project and the paper are mediocre at best, despite the hours of effort you put into them.

Your parents then forced you to take a nap. You have just awakened, still tired, and it's early Sunday evening. You stare at your theology textbook while preparing for Monday's test. After about an hour, the sentences on the page wave like the waters on the ocean. You grab a cola from the fridge in hopes that the caffeine will give you a little boost. You turn on the fan. You slap yourself in the face. Nothing seems to help. Still, you press on.

The next thing you know is that a voice is calling your name. You open your eyes to what you think is the large print edition of your theology textbook. You are not sure where you are. In school? At home? Your hear that you are going to be late for football practice. What? You realize that you fell asleep studying for your test. You are late for practice and still not ready for your test. Your neck aches from sleeping with your head on the desk and you are exhausted. Then you lose it. First you fling the soft drink can across the room. You rip a poster off the wall. Words come out of your mouth that your parents don't think you know. Before your parents come in to discover the source of the commotion, you kick a hole in the wall.

Now you've really done it. Besides being late for football practice, you will fail your theology test, get an F for your project and paper, and get grounded for destroying your bedroom. You sink into misery and think, "I just can't do it all."

How to Handle the Situation

Realizing that you cannot do it all alone is not a failure but the beginning of success. The faster you realize this truth, the better off you will be. What follows are some attractive approaches to avoid attempting an amassed amount of actions alone.

 Thinking that you can do it alone is a big, sad ego trip.

- The best leaders are listeners. The best leaders coordinate with and work with others. The best leaders encourage and motivate those they work with to do their best.
- Think about this. After college, you will do few things alone. Raising a family, running a business, and almost every other major endeavor in life require numerous people working together to achieve success. The next time you watch a movie, also watch the credits roll on the screen and count how many people it took to produce the movie.

 Your parents are there for you.

- Relying on your parents is not a sign of weakness but a sign of a family's strength.
- Independence is good, but there is a fine line between youthful stoicism and a healthy reliance on your

parents. Independence is something that both you and your parents will have to patiently work through.

 ## Other family members are there for you.

- Your older brothers and sisters have been there before. Seek their advice. Check with your aunts, uncles, and cousins too. You probably have a lot of experience at your fingertips.

 ## Your teachers, coaches, and counselors are there for you.

- When you get overwhelmed, make sure you talk to the people who can have a direct impact on the situation. A teacher can grant you an extension on a paper or offer additional help. A coach can excuse you from a practice. Ask. The worst they can do is say no.
- Here's how to ask a teacher for an extension: "Hi, Mr./Mrs./Ms. (insert name). I know that my paper is due next Monday. I really want to give it the time and attention it deserves, but I have (insert name of the other tests, projects, and so on) due on that day. Can I please have an extension on the due date for your paper?" Gathering a number of other students in the same predicament to make the appeal might also have a strong effect (but make sure you do not appear to be ganging up on the teacher).

Your friends are there for you.

- Sometimes just talking about your pressures can help relieve them a little. Certainly some of your friends are feeling the same things. Don't be afraid to seek consolation and support from your friends.
- Your friends might also have some suggestions. Maybe they have been in the same situation and can offer some solutions.

 ## God is there for you.

- In the midst of problems, you can take comfort in knowing that God is there for you. So when you do not know a way out of your problems, ask God for help.
- "For God all things are possible" (Mark 10:27).
- "Who will separate us from the love of Christ? Will hardship, or distress, or persecution, or famine, or nakedness, or peril, or sword? No . . . for I am convinced that neither death, nor life, nor angels, nor rulers, nor things present, nor things to come, nor powers, nor height, nor depth, nor anything else in creation, will be able to separate us from the love of God in Christ Jesus our Lord" (Romans 8:35,37–39).

Don't let one mistake overshadow all that is
good in your life.

One Mistake Is Not the End of the World

I do not understand my own actions. For I do not do what I want, but I do the very thing I hate. (Romans 7:15)

Return to the LORD, your God,
    for he is gracious and merciful,
slow to anger, and abounding in steadfast love,
    and relents from punishing.

(Joel 2:13)

Situation

Here is the myth that so many ninth-grade students believe: *All mistakes will ultimately result in my becoming penniless and alone.* It is as though their minds become Formula One race cars and take off without their permission. If you never make a mistake—great! Hopefully you never will, but someday you might. So consider the following few situations in which you might find yourself.

You have failed a test. Your mind races to the next logical scenario: you are now probably in danger of failing the class. "Oh no!" you think. "I can't fail. I need to go to college." Your mind kicks the speed up a notch and then you are off in the Mindrace 500! Your brain has become a Formula One car, busting out 19,000 rpms of pure neurotransmitting brainpower. You take the first turn around the cerebral cortex and come to the conclusion that this F will prevent you from getting into college. "Noooo!" you think as you hit the gearshift and crank your brain into overdrive. You race between two receptor cells and try to dodge the neurotraffic coming up from behind, but no, your car is spinning out of control. You now conclude that no college means a crummy job and . . . oh no! You spin around and crash into the parietal lobe. The crummy job will result in misery, which will lead to losing that job and ultimately leaving you penniless and alone—all because you failed the test!

A few weeks later, you have a trio of tests in a single day. Despite knowing that you will have three tests in one day, you wait too long to start studying, which leaves you with far less preparation time than you needed. You barely even start covering the basics of two of the subjects when, at about 12:30 a.m. on the morning of the tests, you begin studying for your biology test. By 1:00 a.m. you lose consciousness and are drooling on the mitosis illustration on your textbook page. The next morning, right before school in a moment of panic, you decide to make a cheat sheet.

In biology class, your anxiety gives you away because you constantly look up to see where the teacher is situated in the classroom. Your teacher notices your upper lip's nervous twitch (the twitch that makes you look like Elvis on too much caffeine). The first time you try to peek at your cheat sheet, the teacher turns around. You're caught! "Oh no," you think. "I'm doomed!" And Mindrace 500 is back on! You hop back into your Formula

One mind car and take an early lead by zooming right past "I will be expelled" and "My parents are going to kick me out of the house" and straight into "I will have a crummy job for the rest of my life." As you speed around the tricky turns of the hypothalamus, you crash into the walls of "Then my boss will hear about how I cheated, and he'll probably fire me from that crummy job." You try to escape this predicament but get caught in the basal ganglia and finally resolve yourself to a penniless and solitary life—all because you cheated.

The final situation is simple. You failed a class. There is no Mindrace 500, no Formula One mind car, no thought processes involved. Your parents have told you since throughout your school career that "if you fail a class, you will eventually become penniless and alone." The final outcome is elementary—you are doomed.

How to Handle the Situation

Despite the awful scenarios your mind concocts and the deterrents that your parents might use to encourage your studies, your world will not come to an end if you make a mistake. Many fine students have been caught cheating and yet still graduated at the top of their class. Other students have failed a class but have gone to graduate from high school and college to enjoy a successful life. Do not get the idea that there won't be any consequences for your shortcomings—there will be. The point is that these events do not have to define you. What *will* define you is *how* you handle these events when they happen.

Notice when your mind is racing, and calm down.

- A natural reaction is to think the worst. It is the defense system in your mind gearing up for all the possible problems ahead. You can almost hear your brain say: "We have a breach in quadrant 1405 and we are moving our readiness up to DEFCON 2. Please stand ready and alert until further instructions."
- When you notice your mind racing, stop and breathe. That's right—stop and breathe. Focus on each breath going in and out of your body. If your mind starts racing again, just return to your breathing . . . in and out. Try it. It really helps your mind slow down.
- After your mind has quit racing, try writing down your options. Putting your thoughts on paper might help you become a little more objective about whatever dilemma you are facing.

 Most people will not judge you.

- In this sense, *to judge* means to deem as being a good or bad person. Most teachers and school administrators have dealt with enough cheaters to know that they are not bad people. They are just people who have had a lapse in judgment. An important tenet of the Catholic faith is that all people are essentially good, even those who have been caught cheating on a test.
- This is not to say that people will not deem the act wrong, especially in the case of cheating. There will be

consequences for your actions, but as the old saying goes, we should "hate the sin, not the sinner."

It takes more than one swing to strike out.

- Getting kicked out of a Catholic school for disciplinary reasons is usually the last step in a process that often includes repeated warnings, detentions, parent meetings, suspensions, and other disciplinary actions. Teachers and administrators know that any student can make a single wrong choice. Being expelled for disciplinary reasons is usually the result of many choices, not just one lapse in judgment.
- A few pretty serious deeds will get you kicked out of a Catholic school for the first offense. If you want to know what they are, look in your student handbook. They are probably listed there.
- If you experience academic difficulties, here's what will help you stay in school: noticeable effort to do honest, hard work. Both teachers and administrators will move heaven and earth for students who are doing their best.

Admit your mistakes and faults.

- Admitting the error of your ways is a sign of maturity and growth. No one is perfect. Acting like you are perfect is a sure sign that you are not.
- When you are mature enough to admit your mistakes and faults, you will gain the respect of your teachers.

You are less likely to be labeled a cheater when you come clean and fess up.

Seek forgiveness.

- If you have cheated, tell the teacher that you are sorry for your deception and that it will not happen again. You will most likely gain your teacher's respect, especially if you follow through on your promise.
- Celebrate the sacrament of Penance and Reconciliation. God's forgiveness is always there for you.

Do not let it drag you down.

- After you have admitted messing up, after you have asked for forgiveness, and after you have vowed never to do it again, let it go. Do not let yourself be burdened by the past.

Curing the Cooties

Let us therefore no longer pass judgment on one another, but resolve instead never to put a stumbling block or hindrance in the way of another. (Romans 14:13)

Heed the counsel of your own heart,
    for no one is more faithful to you than it is.

(Sirach 37:13)

Situation

"Cooties!" you cry. "Jonathan said that I have *cooties,* but it's not true!" You cry for another ten minutes to your mother, who is patiently listening to her seven-year-old's lament about another tough day in first grade. For some reason, your friend (or maybe we should say *ex*-friend) Jonathan has deemed you to be untouchable because you are suffering from the dreaded cooties contamination.

Your wise mother exhibits her years of experience in scientific inquiry by asking the one question that stops you your tracks and gives you reason for a thoughtful pause. She says, "Darling, what *are* cooties and how did you get them?"

What? What kind of question is that? The tears stop. Aha! Maybe your mom has broken through. This momentary probe into logic and reason has forced you to pause and think about this so-called cootie infestation. Your mind begins its analysis: "What are cooties? I can't see them. Are they real, then? Maybe their lack of physical manifestation points to its truly absent existential nature." But then you come to your senses and scream your reply to your mother's question, "Because Jonathan said that I have cooties!"

Cooties are the plague from which you were healed a number of years ago. Or were you? It's possible that your cootie infestation, so well diagnosed by your friend Jonathan, has evolved into a more subtle form of the disease. A closer look into the cootie phenomenon may reveal some useful information for your current ailment.

Cooties are a malady visible only to those who seem to want to embarrass or hurt you. Cooties have no known effect on victims, other than the harm inflicted by the comments of those who claim to see them. Children have tried for years to come up with a cure for cooties. These have been mostly verbal medicines used by the victims on those who discovered the cooties: "Yeah? Well, you're ugly!" "You ARE a cootie!" Unfortunately, these attempts usually make the cootie infestation spread.

The only remedy that makes the cooties go away is an experimental medical procedure that requires the victim to ignore the person who discovers the cooties. Pretty soon the cooties just seem to drift away and become a distant memory.

Obviously, if someone were to say that you have cooties now, you would laugh at them and walk away. It would be laughable to give such an accusation even a slight acknowledgement. The person who is claiming that you have cooties would be considered childish and an embarrassment to all who know that person.

Back to your current crisis. The cooties have apparently mutated into a more subtle form of peer criticism, but remember this: the remedy is still the same.

Another illness, similarly discovered, has different symptoms. The primary symptom is a continual swollen head. As opposed to cooties, this ailment begins with compliments and congratulatory statements like, "Great job at the game last night!" or "I'll bet you will get a scholarship." Apparently this ailment is cured by injecting a sense of gratitude combined with a steady dose of humility. With continual treatments, the head should reduce its swelling and return to normal size.

How to Handle the Situation

The words from your peers can be powerful. They can boost you to the tops of mountains or send you to the lowest depths of the valley. Although good, honest, constructive criticism can be helpful and should receive your attention, too often you and your peers are pelted by insults and abuse that sink their sharp claws into your soul and do not let go.

On the other hand, sometimes your wounded spirit allows itself to rise up on the compliments and praise of others. Your popularity inflates your self-esteem until, like a drug addict searching for a fix, you constantly look for affirmation from other people and sink into depression when you do not get it.

There are ways to deal with the comments of your peers, both the positive and the negative ones. What follows are just a few suggestions.

Everyone has an opinion.

- Sometimes opinions are important, and it is good to listen to them. If you take your car to a mechanic, his opinion about your car is valuable. Some folks can offer wisdom about other people. Some examples are psychologists, spiritual directors, and wise grandparents. If you want an opinion that matters, go to the experts you love and trust.
- Everyone is entitled to an opinion. If you think about opinions in terms of supply and demand, most opinions are probably not worth very much. If anyone can make an opinion at no cost, then they are worth nothing—like air. A good opinion requires time, energy, knowledge, understanding, and talent, so be choosy about whose advice you decide to take.

Take it with a grain of salt.

- "Taking it with a grain of salt" means that you do not take the advice or opinions of others too seriously. You listen, but do not accept the advice without some thought and consideration on your part.
- The grain of salt analogy applies to both insults and compliments. We can take both to heart too much sometimes. God gave you both a brain and a heart.

Consider the thoughts and opinions of others, but do not stow them away into your heart as the gospel truth without some of your own reflection first.

Know thyself.

- If you know that the sky is blue but someone tells you that it is red, would you believe that person? Of course not. If someone tells you that you are a jerk, a loser, a wimp, would you believe that person? You may know that the sky is blue, but do you really know who you are?

- One of the problems with knowing who you are is that during high school, you are rapidly changing. So keeping in touch with who you are is important. This requires some quiet time—alone. Journaling, prayer, and other solitary activities will help you know yourself.

- Do not let others define who you are. Even when the defining is offered with good intentions, it can be limiting. Your mother thinks that you will be a great accountant. Your friends think that you are beautiful enough to be a model. You coaches think that you have a future in sports. Your love interest thinks that you would be a good catch. Your priest thinks that the religious life would be perfect for you. Do not ignore these voices, but also do not let them decide who you are. That job is up to you and God alone.

"Heed the counsel of your own heart,
  for no one is more faithful to you than it is.
For our own mind sometimes keeps us better
    informed
  than seven sentinels sitting high on a
    watchtower.
But above all pray to the Most High
  that he may direct your way in truth."

(Sirach 37:13–15)

⚠ You need to please only one person.

- No, that person is not you.
- That person is also not your parents or your friends or your teachers or your priest or your cousin or . . .
- The only person you need to please is God, but the nice part is that pleasing God also makes you a happier person. That doesn't mean that you will win the lottery or earn an A on every test. It means that you will have true satisfaction in life.
- Pleasing God is not always easy or fun, but it does make life better for you and everyone you come into contact with. Pleasing God takes prayer, which helps you know God's will. Prayer also gives you the courage to do what is difficult. Prayer keeps you connected with God. So pray!

Part VI
The Weebles in Your Life

So God created humankind in his image,
> in the image of God he created them;
> male and female he created them.

(Genesis 1:27)

The LORD saw that the wickedness of humankind was great in the earth, and that every inclination of the thoughts of their hearts was only evil continually. And the LORD was sorry that he had made humankind on the earth, and it grieved him to his heart (Genesis 6:5–6).

Weebles Wobble

The Bible has seventy-two books. In these books are 1,309 chapters, which fill up nearly 1,500 pages of small print (depending, of course, on the translation and the edition you have). In the very first chapter of the very first book (Genesis) of the Bible, God looks at all Creation and exclaims what beautiful and special creatures humans are. God seems to ooze with pride over his creation—they were perfect, just like him. But by chapter 6 of that same book, the Lord is totally frustrated with his creation and regrets ever having made humans (see the quotations that begin this introduction). And more than 1,300 chapters in the Bible are left to go. If God has a tough time dealing with his human creation, do not feel bad if you have the same difficulties.

What's interesting is that the Bible passages noted are *both* true. Humans are made in God's image, yet at the same time, human beings have separated themselves from the perfection they once experienced. Among them, no person is fully good, and no one is fully bad.

Remember Weebles? They are still around. They are little human-like toys with round, weighted bottoms that rock back and forth when the toy is pushed. Weebles rock all the way to one side but soon come rushing back the other way, too far the other way to stand straight. It is almost impossible to get a Weeble to stand straight. Similarly, everyone wobbles back and forth trying to get life right. At times, some do better than others; some do worse. Nonetheless, everyone is flawed to some degree. This includes your peers, your parents, and your teachers.

Also interesting is that Weebles never fall down. Similarly, people have that divine perfection in them— that spark of essential goodness that can never be taken away. You'll find that spark in your best friend who listens to you when you are down, in your mom and dad who take care of you, and in your little brother who stole the loose change from your dresser drawer last week. It is also in your biology teacher who would not accept your late homework assignment and even in the bully who used to pick on you when you were younger.

The spark of goodness is in you too, even when you do not always do the right thing. Recall the worst thing you have ever done. Despite that, you still are made in the image and likeness of God. Nothing can take that away from you.

What You Will Find in This Section

High school is full of Weebles. As you wobble back and forth between the good and not-so-good things that you do, try to remember that everyone is wobbling. Like you, they have the spark of God firing within them, and like you, they forget about this—even adults like your parents and teachers forget. Have some compassion for your fellow wobbling human beings out there. In this section, you will find information to ease your interactions with people you encounter in high school.

- Understanding Your Parents
- Teachers Are Not All Alike
- Negotiating Peer Politics

NOTES

Parents and kids can view the same situation
in very different ways.

Understanding Your Parents

"Honor your father and your mother, so that your days may be long in the land that the Lord your God is giving you" (Exodus 20:12).

"I have not come to bring peace, but a sword.
    For I have come to set a man against his father,
    and a daughter against her mother."

(Matthew 10:34–35)

Your Parents: An Insider's Look

When actors want to "get inside" a particular role, one method they use is to try to understand the motives of the characters they are to portray. In most cases, those motives are not written plainly in the script, so the actors have to investigate between the lines to learn what makes characters do what they do.

For example, let's say that an actor believes that the character he is playing is planning to rob a bank only because he wants to impress his older brother. The actor's facial expressions and body language would then reveal his need for his brother's acceptance and approval. On the other hand, if the actor believes that the character is robbing the bank out of greed and malice, his portrayal would be different. Exploring a character's motives gives the actor a deeper understanding of why people do what they do.

Exploring the motives of the people in your life can offer you similar benefits. First, it is important to accept that you cannot read other people's minds, nor can you ever truly know what motivates another's actions. Sometimes it is difficult to know it even within yourself. Saint Paul said: "I do not understand my own actions. For I do not do what I want, but I do the very thing I hate" (Roman 7:15). Nonetheless, acknowledging and respecting the limitations of investigating the motivations of others can be a valuable activity.

Understanding what motivates your parents is one of the keys to a harmonious relationship with them. No two parents are alike. They might all have different motivations, but when it comes to their children, they have love and fear in common. It is pretty safe to say that almost all of a parent's decisions are based on these two strong emotions. If you take this into consideration when dealing with your parents, life for you (and them) will be so much easier.

Generally speaking, your parents love you. They work hard to put food on the table, give you shelter, make sure that you are well educated, offer you life-enhancing experiences such as sports and hobbies, and do many more things too numerous to include here. Because of this love, your parents often make many sacrifices for you. They give up time to drive you places, help with homework, meet with your teachers, and so on. They pay tuition to send you to a private school rather than to a no-cost public school. They take you to church and are the first ones to teach you the difference between right and wrong.

Teenagers' conflicts with their parents often occur because of what parents fear. Why are they scared? They are scared because there is nothing worse than losing a child, but mostly because they want you to be safe and happy. They love you more than anything. They know that teenagers sometimes take unnecessary risks. What do they fear? That depends on the parent, but here is a general list that will cover the worries of most parental units.

Parents worry that

- you will be hurt in a tragic car accident.
- you will hurt someone else in a tragic car accident.
- they are giving you too much attention.
- they are not giving you enough attention.
- you will get involved in the wrong crowd and do drugs.
- you will not handle peer pressure well.
- you will not focus on your studies enough.
- you will focus too much on your studies.
- you will graduate and move far away to go to college.
- you will fail out of high school, never go to college, and will have to live with them for the rest of their lives.
- a meteor might fall from the sky smack dab into your forehead.
- all of their anxieties and worries are warping your youthful soul.

Some of these worries may seem absurd to you. It makes no sense that parents simultaneously worry that their child is focusing too much on studies and that their child is not focusing enough. Worries do not have to make sense, and these fears are quite real for your parents. They are real because your parents remember what it was like in high school. Some things have changed, but many things have not.

How to Work with Your Parents

Your parents are still learning how to be parents, especially if you are the oldest or only child. Even if they act like they know everything, they do not. (If you are wise, you will act like you never heard this before.) Like you, they are doing something they have never done before. Even if you have had three older siblings go through high school, the experience is still different with every child. Parents are not always sure what to do (but remember that many times, they are). Try to have some sympathy and compassion for their situation. It will help everyone in the long fun.

 Be safety-conscious.

- If you show your parents that you are truly conscious of your safety, they will most likely begin to trust you more. As you probably know, with your parents' trust comes many benefits.
- Try not to act annoyed about having to call your parents when you arrive and leave places. This quick deed can help calm their anxieties immensely.
- You have just one reason for being safety-conscious: it helps keep you healthy and alive. Above anything else, this is what your parents want for you.

 Ask your parents about their experiences in high school.

- Ask them to be honest about where they went wrong. Find out about the lessons they learned. Isn't it better to learn from other people's mistakes rather than your own?

- Talking with your parents about their high school experiences might help you discern their current motivations. Parents often work hard so that you do not make the same mistakes they did. If your dad was in a car accident in high school, it might explain why he is so sensitive when it comes to your driving now.
- Here is a question that will spark a good conversation: "Mom (or Dad), what experiences did you have in high school that affect how you parent me now?"

Talk to your parents.

- Keeping parents up to date about your personal life will ease their worries. If you think about it, you benefit in the long run too. The less they worry, the more privileges you might earn, right?
- Though they may seem like the geekiest people in the world, and probably the ones least able to help, your parents might occasionally let a few gems of wisdom fall from their lips. Your parents want to help and are there for you. Talk to them.
- In appropriate circumstances, be willing to offer and make deals with your parents. For instance, you might hate talking to your parents on the phone when your friends are around. If your parents agree to keep the calls short and sweet, promise to call when you arrive and leave a location without their nagging. Think of other ways you can give and take that will make everyone happier.
- An older sibling's trouble in high school will hopefully not affect your parents' attitudes toward you. If you feel like you are suffering for the wrongdoings of your siblings, though, be sure to talk to your parents about it.

Teachers, like everyone else, come in all shapes and sizes
and with different personalities.

Teachers Are Not All Alike

Though the LORD may give you the bread of adversity and the water of affliction, yet your Teacher will not hide himself any more, but your eyes shall see your Teacher. And when you turn to the right or when you turn to the left, your ears shall hear a word behind you saying, "This is the way; walk in it" (Isaiah 30:20–21).

Who Are Your High School Teachers?

You have probably heard this warning more times in eighth grade than you care to remember—and it most likely came from several of your teachers' mouths: "Wait till you get into high school!" This ominous reprimand was probably followed by one of these gems: "You won't have me to hold your hand," or "The teachers won't be as nice and forgiving as I am," or "They won't let you go back to your locker to get your homework," (or your book, your pen, your lunch, or the earplugs you desperately want so you can drown out your teacher's complaints).

Are these warnings true? Should you be worried about the disposition of your high school teachers? Will they allow you to do the things your junior high teachers allowed you to do? The answer is simple: yes and no. In general, they will expect you to be more responsible and hold you to a higher standard than you had in junior high. You will have numerous teachers with their own personalities and possibly wildly different demands.

Some will be very strict in terms of discipline. Some will not. Some will give you a hall pass to go back and get the book you forgot. Some will not.

Your high school teachers are as diverse as any other group of people. Although some people have the notion that teachers at Catholic schools are either priests or nuns, this is not the case. In fact, you will find that most of your teachers are lay people (those who are not ordained into the priesthood).

In your high school career you will have both male and female teachers. Your teachers will be Democrats, Republicans, and Independents. They will come in all sorts, shapes, and sizes. Many will be Catholic, but a number of them will not be. One teacher might spend a lot of time answering your questions, while others might make you answer their questions. You will have both unforgettable and forgettable teachers. Some will bore you to tears, while others will inspire you to move mountains. You will have every kind of teacher under the sun in your four years of high school.

How to Work with Your Teachers

One of the challenges of high school is to learn how to deal with the different demands of your instructors. Keep in mind that you cannot generalize about a group of people, nor can you expect them to react the same way to every event. But what follows here are a few basic good rules to remember for dealing with your teachers.

Personal issues need to be addressed outside of class.

- Sometimes teachers will use time during class to offer individual attention to students, but this will probably not be the norm.
- In general, your teachers need to spend class time educating everyone in the class. This does not mean that you cannot ask questions. On the contrary, you should ask questions when you have them, but if you have an issue that requires a lot of time, save it for later.
- When you need help, ask for it. Teachers are more than happy to address your problems before or after school. Do not be afraid to ask. Sometimes teachers will set aside regular times before or after school for students to drop in to see them.
- Let's pretend that you are having problems in your algebra class. Here is a good way to address your issue: "Hi, Mr. Johnson! I am having a problem understanding (insert problem). Do you have a few minutes sometime in the near future to go over this with me again?"
- Do not wait until it is too late to ask for help. If you are confused about something, do not put it off until the day before the test to say to your algebra teacher: "Mr. Jackson, I don't understand that thing you were talking about two weeks ago. And I haven't really understood anything since then either. Can you stay after school to help me?" Oh no. That will *not* go over well.

 Teachers do not "give" grades.

- One of the teacher's main jobs is to assess the work you have done (a paper, test, project, and so on) and assign a grade that reflects your mastery of that particular task or body of knowledge. Do not ever ask a teacher, "Why did you give me this grade?" They did not "give" it to you. Grades just reflect the work that was done.

- If you honestly do not know why you received a lower grade than you expected, ask the teacher to explain *how he or she arrived at your grade* and *what you could have done better* to receive a higher one.

- If you think the teacher has made a mistake in grading, do not get angry. Teachers are only human and make honest mistakes sometimes. Calmly point out the mistake or your reasons why you think the grade was a mistake, and the teacher will usually be very happy to change it or explain the reason for the grade.

Stay on topic.

- One sure-fire way to annoy your teacher (and probably most of your classmates) is to ask questions or comment on something that has no relation to the topic you are currently exploring. Consider this scenario: You are studying Jesus's parables in your theology class. You raise your hand and ask, "Do you think that Jesus ever went on a date?"

- Keep your comments and questions relevant to the discussion.

Ask good questions.

Consider these rules:

- A good question has not already been answered. Pay attention.

- A good question makes people think.
- A good question keeps the conversation going.
- A good question exhibits your current understanding, as well as what you do not know or understand.
- When you do not understand something, try asking your teacher to compare it to something more familiar to you and your classmates. Or ask for the opposite. Find creative ways that will help your instructor to clarify the topic at hand.

Teaching is a hard job.

- Although teaching is one of the most important jobs in any society, teachers are often not given the respect and compensation that they deserve.
- Not only do teachers work all day, they also take work home. They spend many hours grading papers, tests, and projects, as well as preparing for their next classes. They also have lives of their own (families, hobbies, volunteering, and so on). Make sure you have reasonable expectations about the time it takes to get your graded work backgraded. Depending on the situation, a week might be an acceptable amount of time for your teachers to return a graded test.
- Be sure to thank your teachers. Make a point to stop at the end of each semester or year and thank them for teaching you. You might not realize until college or later on in life the impact they had on you. When this happens, drop by or write a note to thank them. It will truly make their day.

Choose friends that challenge you to be a better person.

Negotiating Peer Politics

Limit the time you spend among fools,
but frequent the company of thoughtful men.

(Sirach 27:12, NAB)

Your Peers: Thoughtful and Foolish

The Scripture passage above from Sirach says it all. Nothing needs to be added and so this chapter might seem more or less useless. However, a more thorough explanation might help, so an appeal to some of the various learning styles will be made.

For the mathematically gifted:

person + thoughtfulness = good
person + foolishness = bad

For the spatial thinkers (follow the arrows):

thoughtful people ⟶ you
foolish people ⟶ you

For the cinematically minded:

Obi-wan Kenobi is a thoughtful guy.
Jabba the Hut is a foolish guy.

For the linguistically talented:

Thoughtful people are considerate, prudent, magnanimous, benevolent, accommodating, concerned, forbearing, and chivalrous.

Foolish people are imbecilic, incompetent, puerile, and obtuse.

For the naturalist thinkers:

Thoughtful people are like sunny spring days when it is just warm enough to wear your shorts outside.

Foolish people are like category 5 tornadoes that wipe out entire towns in the Midwest.

Unfortunately, identifying the foolish and thoughtful people does not come easily. One problem you will face is that your peers will often drift from the foolish camp to the thoughtful camp and back again without warning. Bear mind that (despite the disturbing nature of this information) that *you* will also move between these two camps . . . quite often . . . uh . . . okay, at least occasionally . . . at least. It is just human nature.

What psychologists have discovered (and teenagers have always known) is that high school students tend to place a lot of value on what their peers think and say about them. During this time young people seek to identify themselves with a particular clique or group. Being a part of a particular group, whether it is a sports team, a club, or just a collection of friends, is a way of expressing who you are, what you like, your values, your beliefs, or many other aspects of your life.

In and of itself, being part of a group is no problem. In fact, it's normal and healthy. The difficulties arise when certain groups insult or disparage other groups, and people are purposefully and cruelly excluded.

Often, an artificial hierarchy develops in a school with the "cool" people on top and the rest falling underneath in varying degrees. Traditionally the cool people include students who are athletes, cheerleaders, physically attractive, or wealthy. For those outside this group, the cool people appear to have everything. Maybe a guy is dating the most attractive girl on campus. Maybe a girl is the varsity cheerleader and president of the student council. On the surface, they seem to have everything that those outside the group really want. At times, they are the envy of everyone.

In most people, however, you will find substance beyond the outward appearance of good fortune.

Some people are blessed with good looks, talent, resources, and genuine kindness and good-heartedness. You might notice that these admirable people do not confine themselves to a single elite group but move in and out of several different crowds with ease. Their friends are not limited to those popular few at the top of the social heap.

You might also encounter people who lack the integrity of those described in the preceding paragraph. On a superficial level these people seem to have it all, but their lack of maturity is expressed in their need to place themselves above the rest. Their insecurity drives their need for attention and admiration from the rest of the school.

Despite the inclination to believe those who say certain people are outcasts because they are not good enough to be among the "cool," consider this truth: *those who do not need to be a part of that group* are actually the more mature, confident, and self-assured people. Of course, this truth may never be acknowledged by most of your peers, but at least you now know the truth.

How to Navigate Peer Relations

Friends are one reason that high school is such a rewarding experience. But at times, friends can also make high school frustrating beyond belief. As you enter the wonderful world of high school relationships, be sure to have your feet firmly planted on the ground. Below are some socially conscious suggestions for avoiding the perilous pitfalls of peer politics.

The cool group is defined.

- Members are sometimes self-proclaimed, sometimes elected by popular opinion, sometimes associated with the genetic inheritance of physical beauty or athletic prowess, and nearly always the object of jealousy.
- Membership costs sometimes include abandonment of personal viewpoints, extreme physical measures to ensure bodily attractiveness, desertion of old friends (at least the ones that are not cool), anxiety and stress over continuing membership status, and a reduction in cash flow because of spending your part-time paycheck on expensive clothing.
- Benefits might include name recognition, constant association with the clique, relentless exposure to public opinion, inaccurate and vicious gossip about you, friendships based on questionable motives, and no more self-esteem issues because the rest of the world will tell you how good or bad you are.

Still interested in joining?

Do not be a reverse snob.

- Some groups at the top of the social ladder in high school look down on the rest of the masses in self-absorbed pity. This is not good. Some people look down on the social elite with a similar self-consumed pity. This is not good either. Snobbery is snobbery, no matter what direction it flows.
- Everyone has prejudices. The problems come when we *act* on these prejudices without thinking. Classifying people into easily identifiable categories and then labeling and excluding them is wrong. Racism and sexism are clear examples of this. The more subtle prejudices in high school—for example, judging people by the clothes they wear—might be harder to identify, but they are no less wrong.

 ## Take the stress out of peer pressure.

- Think ahead. Have your responses ready for each problem that you will be sure to face with your peers (drugs, alcohol, sex, skipping school, and so on). What will you do when . . . ?
- Feel free to blame your parents. Almost every teenager understands this excuse: "My parents are so strict and they *will* find out . . ."
- Cultivate the habit to think before you act. Try counting to ten before you answer. Your friends might find this habit a little odd, but in some circumstances, it might save your life. Consider the consequences before you jump into a situation.

Know who is a friend.

- Try not to lose your oldest and closest friends. You may grow apart, but try to stay in touch because no one knows you better than the friends who went to your birthday party in first grade when you got so excited over your new bike that you threw up on the cake.
- Those who pressure you to do things that you do not want to do are not true friends. Stay away from them.
- It is also true that friends make mistakes too. Forgiveness is mandatory in friendship. Be sure to offer and to ask for forgiveness.

Things change.

- High school is a time of great change. Shy people become outgoing. Obnoxious people become more introspective. New interests develop. Grades get better . . . or worse. Be ready to see the changes in yourself and in your friends.
- Support your friends when they go through these changes. Encourage their new interests. If your friend wants to join a new club, tell him or her how great you think it is. Even though you are not interested in the club and your friend's joining might mean you'll spend less time together, your support will make your friendship stronger.
- If you see that things are changing for the worse in your friends, do not feel shy about doing something for them. For example, if you see that your friends' grades are declining or that they are getting involved with

drugs, talk to them, their counselor, and their parents. Your friends might not appreciate this kind of help at the time, but later they will probably thank you from the bottom of their hearts.

NOTES

Part VII
Things to Be Excited About

Happy is the person who meditates on wisdom
     and reasons intelligently,
who reflects in his heart on her ways
     and ponders her secrets.

(Sirach 14:20–21)

Yes, We Said "Excited"

Hold on! School? Excitement? Can you say "oxymoron"? No, it does not mean "super-moron!" To make sure everyone is on the same page here, it would be wise to define the term:

> **oxymoron** (awk-see-'mor-on) *n* a phrase in which contradictory terms are used together, for example, *deafening silence, jumbo shrimp,* and *constant variable.*

So, no. It is not an oxymoron. And yes, there are things in high school worthy of your excitement. In fact, here is a list: new friends, new teachers, new classrooms, more options, new place to be, new start, dances, proms, sports, clubs, more freedom, bigger school, no constant teacher escorts, no single-file lines, class choices, new opportunities, freedom from old reputation, and more.

Planting the Right Seeds

In all honesty, one must say that high school will be whatever you make it. If you cultivate the seeds of apple trees, what will most likely shoot up from the ground are apple trees. If you plant and nurture seeds for a banana tree, rarely would a rosebush come from the ground. If anything other than a banana tree grows, it would be only by coincidence. For the most part, your high school experiences will reflect a series of choices you make. If you have a wonderful time in high school, it will not be because of a coincidence.

If you begin high school with an attitude that the experience will be boring and irrelevant, that is most likely what will happen. High school will be boring and irrelevant for you. Even the best teachers cannot make you enjoy their classes. They can only present the material as best they can. The rest is up to you.

But if you are approaching high school as a new beginning with many exciting and adventurous opportunities, that is most likely what it will become for you. This does not mean that every single moment will be like an action-adventure movie, but cultivating a positive attitude will help. So the question for you to answer is, What seeds do you want to plant?

Excitement is on the agenda.

You have the correct tools. You have a great variety of seeds from which to choose. You have been given the time to plant. You have numerous gardening assistants to help you (teachers, counselors, administration, parents). Spring has come and it is time to plant. Being in high school is like having a great weather forecast—just the right mixture of sun and rain. Excitement is on the agenda. All you have to do is add your part. So what will it be?

What You Will Find in This Section

In the following pages you will find several exciting situations and opportunities that you will encounter when you begin high school. Each one is your chance to plant a seed that will grow and nourish your high school experience:

- Meeting New People
- Re-establishing Yourself
- More Interesting Studies
- More Independence

Meeting New People

Pleasant speech multiplies friends,
   and a gracious tongue multiplies courtesies.
Let those who are friendly with you be many,
   but let your advisers be one in a thousand.

(Sirach 6:5–6)

Situation

Imagine that you have walked into the gymnasium for ninth-grade orientation on the first day of high school. The gym is teeming with students whom you have never seen. You—and they—are all in the same situation. On the faces of those around you are different looks, all clues to how each person in the room is anticipating what lies ahead. Some are smiling and bubbly. Some look tough and aloof. Others seem lost, confused, or sad. One face looks like it belongs to a new lottery winner. Another is the look of someone whose life savings have disappeared.

As you take in these new faces, a number of thoughts and emotions might race through your mind and heart: curiosity, excitement, trepidation, anxiety, insecurity, joy, interest, satisfaction, relief, and many more—all at once. Questions will likely pop up into your mind. Who are the people behind these faces? Who will become my friends? Why is that person so happy? Why does she look so miserable? What is his problem? What is her name? Will I like him? Will they like me?

You realize that you will probably spend much of the next four years of your life with these people.

How to Handle the Situation

Imagine that you have left the time-space continuum and are able to look at several different periods of time in your life at once. Note how your perception changes as you grow older and relationships change. Let us take a look at the first day of school and then take a few steps into the future and compare your thoughts about the people you have encountered along the way.

On your first day of ninth grade, you stand in the gymnasium, looking around at all the unfamiliar faces. "That guy looks like a loser," you think as one of your new classmates passes by. Little did you know that "that guy" would become one of your best friends by your senior year. "Ooh!" you gasp as an attractive member of the opposite sex strolls by. Again you do not yet realize that after two years of gawking at this person from afar, you finally land a date . . . and the date goes so badly that by the end of it, you wish you had never even met this person before. Another new classmate passes you by, but you do not notice this person at all. In ninth grade, you did not know that person would someday become your spouse.

One of the biggest worries of ninth graders every-where is "Will they like me?" Knowing the answer seems to calm the nerves of rookie high schoolers, so it is a great honor to provide the answer to you now . . . (hear the drum roll?) . . . and the answer is . . . (more drum rolling) . . . yes *and* no. Yes, some people will like you, and no, some people will not like you. For those who are devastated by the realization that their grandmother has lied to them all these years ("Yes, honey, everyone is going to love you. How could they not?"), feel free to go to the counselors' office for assistance.

It will be a wonderful day when all people can say that they see one another as the image of God in which they were made and that personality differences just make everyone special. Unfortunately, this has never happened to the human race nor will it happen for a long time (aka the Second Coming of Christ). Until then, we have to deal with one another's various temperaments and personal dispositions. So do not expect everyone to like you. Did you like everyone in junior high? High school will be no different.

How do you deal with the oncoming human traffic? How can you meet so many people at once and sort out where you fit into one another's lives? Most of this comes naturally because you have already been doing it in one form or another for a long time, but nonetheless, here are a few words of advice on how to find friends and fend off future formidable foes.

Do not base everything on first impressions.

- First impressions can give you a lot of information, and it is good to listen to your gut instincts, but it is also wise to acknowledge that they might be wrong. Give people more than one chance before you write them off as someone you would rather avoid.
- People have bad days. Imagine if you were to meet a new person the day after your grandfather, whom you loved dearly, passed away. That person might think that you are a morose and depressing person and prefer not

to hang out with you because they would not know that your grandfather just died. Remember that people are not at their best all the time. Give them another chance.

⚠ You are not finished in ninth grade.

- High school will be four years of meeting and getting to know people, both inside and outside your school.
- People change, especially in their high school years. The girl you could not stand in ninth grade might be your best friend in your junior year. People grow, acquire new tastes and hobbies, mature, and change attitudes all the time. The one who changes might be you.

⚠ Use the Internet wisely.

- Making friendships on the Internet is risky, sometimes even life-threatening. You do not always know who you are talking to. The "friend" you met online might be an Internet predator.
- Never, never, never agree to meet someone in person that you met online—without your parents' approval and adult accompaniment.
- Try to avoid Internet friendships—period. People need the human touch that communication through computers cannot provide.
- Even with people you personally know, you cannot always trust the information you get about or from them online. You can never truly say for certain who posted it.

Not all friends are the same.

- Not every person is going to be your best friend and that is fine. You are not going to be everyone's best friend and that is fine too. Try not to expect that.
- You will probably have just a few close friends. You will hang out with a larger circle of friends. You will do only specific things, like hobbies or sporting activities, with some friends. Having lots of different kinds of friends is good. Try not to close yourself into one particular group.

Look behind the masks.

- Everyone wears masks—everyone. This is not to say that everyone is a fake, but all people wear masks that show the world how they want to be seen.
- Among the new people you meet, the ones who let down their masks are the ones who quite often become your best friends. This is good to keep in mind.
- The inverse is also true. If you feel comfortable letting down your mask with someone, that's a good indicator of where that person will fit in your life. Such people can become your best friends.

If you were to poll some adults, you would probably find a few who met their best friends for life in high school. You might also discover that these same adults continued to develop meaningful friendships after high school. High school can be a great time for you to create friendships and acquire the skills to develop meaningful relationships for the rest of your life.

Take the time in high school to find out who you are.

Re-establishing Yourself

Do not remember the former things,
>or consider the things of old.
I am about to do a new thing;
>now it springs forth, do you not perceive it?

>(Isaiah 43:18–19)

Joseph's Situation

Throughout his junior high days at Saint Anne School, Joseph was a constant thorn in the side of his teachers. When he started Saint Anne's in sixth grade, he was going through a tough time in life. His parents had recently divorced and he was living with his mother, who had just moved to the city to take advantage of a business opportunity. Joseph was angry with his parents for splitting up. He was even angrier with his mom for making him move away from his father and his friends at his old school, where he was a notably good student.

Joseph took out his anger on his classes. He refused to do any of his class work and spent most of his class time trying to avoid thinking about everything that made him angry. So he drew pictures, whispered jokes to his pals, and played practical jokes on teachers. His grades fell and his mother received many discipline notices from the teachers about Joseph.

After the first semester in the new school, Joseph went to see a counselor who helped him deal with the things that made him so angry; by the end of sixth grade, he was starting to feel better. Nonetheless, the damage was done. Joseph had already established a pretty negative reputation among the teachers, as well as some not-so-good habits in the classroom. Egged on by his classmates, Joseph got a lot of attention for his classroom antics and continued his poor behavior.

By eighth grade, Joseph's behavior had improved, but he felt that he could not escape his self-made entanglement. Still, he looked ahead to high school and, he thought, his hope.

Malika's Situation

Since first grade, Malika was a shy girl who did well in her studies. In order to avoid drawing attention to herself, she rarely raised her hand in class, so she made sure to pay close attention to teachers' directions. Malika did not make new friends easily. She kept the few close friends that she had and did not move out of that circle very often.

Malika was secretly jealous of other kids who were so comfortable voicing their opinions in class. Her envy extended into the social arena, where she was not as outgoing as the other girls when it came to meeting boys. At school dances, she sat near the edge of the room and never asked a guy to dance. She also refused any requests to join the boys on the dance floor. Malika occasionally joined group dances, where she could blend in with the crowd. She had fun, but she wanted something more.

Malika was bothered by her own shyness. She knew that she was trapped by her own unreasonable fears. Wanting to bust through these fears, she looked for an opening, a chance to become the person she knew she really was. Malika looked ahead to high school, where she hoped an opportunity to break out awaited her.

How to Handle the Situation

Imagine that you are in a totally different life situation. Nobody knows your name, your background, your personality, your habits, your intelligence, your reputation—nothing. All the people with you in this situation are starting with a blank slate. You can become anyone you want to be. You can walk in, greet everyone, and say that you grew up in the wilds of Africa, where you spent much of your childhood as a bee hunter. You can say that your father is an entomologist who studied the particular breeds of bees that live in Africa. You can say that on weekends you earned extra cash by hunting and capturing the bees for your father's study. If you have a scar, you can point to it and say that you were stung there by a giant antelope-eating bee.

You might get a few raised eyebrows, but the people you tell your story to would not know anything different. Yes, your tale-telling would be lying and immoral, and no, you should never lie, but you get the idea, right? *They have no idea who you are.* You just might be a bee hunter from the wilds of Africa—and who is there to say anything different?

Starting high school can be a special opportunity that comes every so often in life—a fresh start. Compare it to having your record wiped away when you move to a town where no one knows you. Odds are that at least a companion or two from your old school has moved on to the same high school with you, but the idea still applies. Personality changes are even expected among your peers. No one really thinks that you will stay the same person that you were in junior high. Think about it. Are all your friends the same as they were in fourth grade?

This is a special opportunity for you because you can make a *conscious decision* to become who you really are. What follows are some hints to help you satisfactorily situate yourself at school.

 ## You can step out of your older sibling's footsteps.

- If your teachers constantly compare you with your older sibling, politely ask them to stop. They should not be doing it anyway. If you have to, show them this book.
- Have some patience. Even though you might get a few comparisons early on, you will establish your own reputation pretty quickly. Teachers tend to catch on to the differences in short order.

 ## Make sure the "new you" is the *real* you.

- Before you do anything make sure you *want* to change. Sometimes people are happy as they are. If it ain't broke, don't fix it.
- Do not mistake being more *outgoing* with being more *popular.* Think about it—there is a big difference.
- Wanting to leave your old self behind is sometimes a natural thing to do, but those seeking to become more popular will often try to become someone they are not. Do not be a fake in order to receive attention,

admiration, or popularity. The fakery will only come back to haunt you.

 ## Try new things.

- Sometimes you do not know whether you like something until you try it. You'll be amazed at what you will like.
- Try something outside of your normal range of activities. If you are into sports, try an artistic activity. If you like the performing arts, check out the science clubs. If you like to just stay home and watch television, get a life. (See Part II: "So Many Options, So Little Time.")

 ## What if you do not know who you are or who you want to be?

- Actually, this is pretty typical for people in high school, so do not freak out. It is a normal stage in life. In fact you will probably have a similar experience in your mid- or late twenties and again in your late forties or early fifties.
- Try not to worry too much. Confusion about your own identity is actually a healthy sign that you are maturing. Oh, what joy, huh?
- This period can actually be very fruitful if you set aside time to focus on prayer, reading the Bible, journaling, creative writing, service work, or other activities that might help you get you out of yourself.
- If you become depressed or overwhelmed, make sure you talk to your parents, a teacher, or a school counselor. Their job is to be there for you.

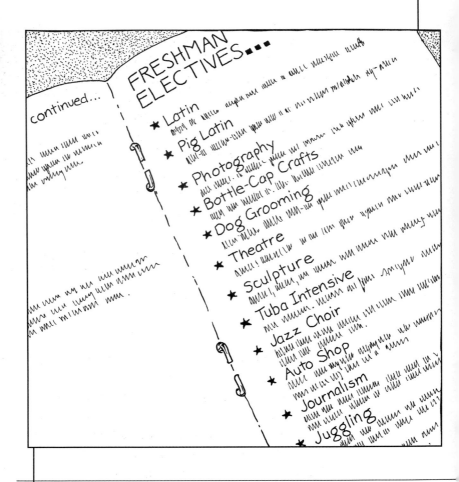

continued...

FRESHMAN ELECTIVES...

★ Latin
★ Pig Latin
★ Photography
★ Bottle-Cap Crafts
★ Dog Grooming
★ Theatre
★ Sculpture
★ Tuba Intensive
★ Jazz Choir
★ Auto Shop
★ Journalism
★ Juggling

Electives are a great way to experience new
and interesting things.

More Interesting Studies

If you love to listen, you will gain knowledge,
> and if you pay attention you will become wise.

Stand in the company of the elders.
> Who is wise? Attach yourself to such a one.

Be ready to listen to every godly discourse,
> and let no wise proverbs escape you.

If you see an intelligent person, rise early to visit him;
> let your foot wear out his doorstep.

(Sirach 6:33–36)

Situation

You have just finished junior high school, where so much was already decided for you. In some cases your freedom of choice was limited, even to whether you wanted creamy or crunchy peanut butter on your sandwich. Now you are signing up for your first year of high school and you are presented with some elective classes.

Wait! What was that? Elective classes? What in the world is an elective class? First, let's look at the definition of *elective:*

> **elective** (i-'lek-tiv) **1** optional **2** that for which one is able to choose **3** an academic class not crammed down your throat by parents, teachers, or any administrative personnel **4** usually a pretty cool class that is full of students who actually *want* to be there.

Sound pretty good? Then read on.

Generally speaking, Catholic high schools are larger than their junior high counterparts, which enables them to offer a broader spectrum of classes. Unless you attend a small school, you will most likely have a choice between several language classes (Spanish, French, Latin, and so on), different kinds of fine arts (music, drawing, painting, photography), and advanced classes for subjects like science, history, and math. (For those of you who were counting on signing up for basket weaving, maybe college will be more obliging.) Although you will be able to choose to take many of these classes, you must score high on the entrance exam or have made exceptional grades in a particular subject to take an advanced class in that subject.

The great thing is that the further you get into high school the more diverse and interesting the classes get. Juniors and seniors can usually choose from classes with names like Healing Racism or World Religions for theology electives, Environmental Science or Oceanography for science electives, Creative Writing or Journalism for English electives, and many, many others (Speech, Jazz Band, Theater, Sculpture, Holocaust Studies, and Computer Programming).

Quite often in one of these classes, you will find students and teachers who are genuinely interested in the subject, which makes for a stimulating and refreshing environment. The atmosphere is sometimes more relaxed because teachers have less arm-twisting to do to keep their students' attention.

If you did not like junior high school, or if you have written off school to be an eternal candidate for "The

Most Boring Thing You Can Do" contest, high school is the time to give it another chance. Quite often (but admittedly not always), classes are more interesting and more relevant to you when you get into high school. College is no longer an event in the faraway future, but instead is an upcoming matter about which you will soon be making decisions. What you do now can really impact your future.

Not only that, but as you get older, your tastes and interests change. Subjects that once were a sleep fest for you might now spark your curiosity and attention. Having a completely new group of teachers also helps. Just getting to know them will be interesting.

How to Handle the Situation

What classes should you register for? Really, your choices should be based on what interests you. Is oceanography a topic you might enjoy? If you are interested in becoming a newspaper writer, then journalism might be a wise choice. Talk to your counselor, teachers, or parents about it if you do not have any idea about what to take. Your counselors will be especially good at advising you (it's their job). They sometimes offer personality tests that can help you identify the fields in which people like you thrive — people with the same particular likes, dislikes, gifts, and talents as you.

Regardless of who helps you, spend some thought and effort on planning your academic future. An array of advanced approaches appropriate for admirably arranging your academic activities follows.

⚠ Find out what classes are available at your school.

- At the beginning of each school year, schools typically distribute handbooks listing all the classes. This is the place to start. If your school does not have such a handbook, ask your counselor or someone in the school's main office for a copy of the curriculum that contains descriptions of the classes offered, including the electives.

- A good way to help you decide what classes you want to take is to browse through the course descriptions to see which ones catch your eye. Read about the classes, and if one sounds interesting, investigate. Ask the teacher of that class or your counselor about the course.

⚠ Plan ahead.

- Some of the most interesting classes have prerequisites. This means that you have to take another class before you are allowed to take that one. For example, if you want to take oceanography, you might have to take another science class first. You might have to take Fundamentals of Art before you can take Sculpture.

- Some classes are only offered occasionally, especially the ones that do not attract a large number of students. For example, a ceramics class may be offered only once every two years. Some classes are only offered in either the spring or fall semesters. Make sure you are aware of these possible restrictions so you are not disappointed.

Only you can determine the best classes to take.

- Your interests are going to be the best judge when it comes to making this decision, so that should be foremost in your consideration. Nonetheless, read on for a few hints to help you decide.
- Who is teaching the class? This is an important question to ask because a good teacher can make a boring subject interesting. Crummy teachers can also make an intriguing topic a complete drag. If you can find out something about the instructor who is teaching the class, that is a good step toward making your decision.
- Ask other students who have already taken the class. Do not just ask them whether they liked it. What you think is good might be completely different from your friends' opinions. Be sure to ask them about specifics like, "Did you have tests or projects or essays?" or "Did you do a lot of activities?" or "Did the teacher just talk all the time?" For instance, if it is a photography class, you might ask whether they went on field trips to shoot pictures. Did the teacher evaluate them with tests or with the photos they took? Was the class a hands-on experience, or did it focus more on theories?

Advanced classes are a good deal.

- If you can take an advanced class, go for it. Normally you are not placed in an advanced class unless the school administration thinks you could handle it.
- Advanced classes are more challenging and faster paced than other classes. Both the students and the teachers usually find the challenges more interesting.
- Juniors and seniors can sometimes earn college credit for completing an advanced placement class.

More Independence

All must test their own work; then that work, rather than their neighbor's work, will become a cause for pride. For all must carry their own loads. (Galatians 6:4–5)

Situation

You come home after your first full week of high school. Your mom and dad sit down to dinner with you and ask about your new teachers, whether you made any new friends, whether you like your classes, and lots of other hokey parent questions. After dinner you help clear the table (at least you should, according to your parents' handbook on childrearing, the one gathering dust on their bedside table) and then you hear it. It starts off as a distant whisper but soon roars toward you like a freight train. It's . . . it's . . . the sound of . . . SILENCE! You hear not a sound from the mouths of your parents. Not "Time to do your homework." Not "Did your finish your assignments?" Not "How's that English paper coming along?" Not "Do you need help with that science project?" Not "What is the due date for your history research paper?" Not a word. No questions, inquiries, investigations, reprimands, warnings, or cautionary tales.

Then you begin to worry. Your mind races. "Did they lose their minds? Did they forget about me? Maybe they don't care whether I do well. Did I wear them out in junior high? Is there an odorless gas leak in the house thwarting their ability to think clearly? What is it? Why the silence?"

A few weeks later, you forget to do your theology homework. The teacher approaches your desk to check your work and you acknowledge that you did not complete your assignment. He then says, "Okay," and moves on to the next student.

Hmm. No warnings. No questions. No inquiries. No "Why didn't you do your work?" No "You'll never make it in this school unless you complete your assignments consistently!" He utters none of the questions or warnings the teachers in junior high issued. No reprimands. No . . . hold on . . . wait! This all sounds too familiar. Conspiracy theories creep into your mind. Maybe your teacher has been *talking to your parents.* It must be a plan. They are giving you the "I'll be nice" treatment—a parent's favorite means of psychological warfare. You are on to their ruthless game: if you do something wrong, they are *nice* to you. Such brutality. Never before have such evil plans been hatched. But no, you will not be their fool. You will not stand for any more kind and courteous behavior. You demand that they return to treating you like a child.

How to Handle the Situation

Although some parents do not loosen their grip when their eighth-grade sons and daughters become ninth graders, many do see the entrance into high school as a time to step back and let their offspring fly or flop. Such a change in attitude might mean fewer questions about homework assignments, less nagging, and just a general easing of control. You might also notice this among your teachers. Your first thoughts might be, "Hey! This is great. I can do what I want!"

After a few weeks you might also notice that without mom and dad "breathing down" your neck and without your teachers' constant reminders to turn in your work, the responsibility for getting your work done is squarely on your shoulders. You might let deadlines slip by or find yourself forgetting the things that your parents or teachers once reminded you of (what you used to call nagging). Although you truly enjoy your new freedom, a little part of you might be wishing you were back in eighth grade when things were easier.

On the good side, your work is becoming truly your own. You find greater satisfaction in bringing home a good report card to your parents that says, "See, I can do it on my own." As Saint Paul says in the opening quote of this chapter, your own hard work gives you a sense of pride. Independence, when used wisely, is a wonderful new experience.

But independence has its costs. Everyone has to pay, but there are good and bad ways to make payments. What follows are some savvy suggestions for the serious student striving for solo success.

⚠️ Enjoy your newfound independence.

- When you act responsibly, you enjoy the many benefits of increased independence. Handling yourself maturely now might soon lead to a driver's license and use of the family car. You can almost taste the freedom from your parents' constant watchful eye.
- This is an exciting time of life and a wonderful opportunity for you. Enjoy these new experiences.

⚠️ Take responsibility.

- You may have heard this wise old saying: "With great freedom comes great responsibility." If you want to really embrace your new independence, you need to also embrace your new responsibilities. It is impossible to have one without the other.
- Imagine that you have the ultimate independence—no parents or teachers to tell you what to do. How would things happen in your life? How would you eat? get medicine? provide yourself with shelter and clothing? Think of a line. At one end is the complete dependence of a newborn baby with no responsibilities. At the other end is total independence in which you are completely responsible for yourself. Where do you fall right now?

Complete dependence/ No responsibility   Complete independence/ Full responsibility

⟵————————————————————⟶

There is a safety net (even though it may not feel like it).

- Life as a ninth grader is like being part of a circus trapeze act. You have worked quite awhile in school, but you have always been attached to a harness that keeps you from falling. Starting high school is like removing the harness. If you miss the trapeze, you will fall—there is nothing to keep you up in the air, but try not to worry too much. The net is still there to catch you.
- This net consists of your parents, teachers, counselors, school administrators, friends, and other family members who watch out for you.
- But the idea remains the same: try not to fall.

 ## Learn from your mistakes.

- If you are going to claim your successes, you have to claim your failures too. Admit your mistakes. You will gain a lot of respect from your parents and teachers.
- Being independent does not mean that you have to be perfect. You will make mistakes, but you have choices when you make mistakes. You can learn from them, move forward, and increase your independence, or you can do the opposite.

- Do not wait for others to fix your problem. Take the initiative to make whatever you are doing a success.

⚠ You can still ask for help.

- Having independence does *not* mean that you have to do it alone. It means that you are responsible enough to take care of any problems you might face. If that means asking for assistance, then ask.
- Because your parents and teachers are giving you more slack does not mean that they are not there for you. If you get into a jam, they are there to help. Do not let foolish pride be the reason that you did not achieve your goals.
- Independence is great, but being part of a school means that its members, including you, should help and rely on one another. That is what being part of a community is all about.

Part VIII
Gender-Specific Issues

So God created humankind in his image,
in the image of God he created them;
male and female he created them.

(Genesis 1:27)

Situation

Boys are tough.
Girls are emotional.
Boys are good at math.
Girls are good in the language arts.

Have you ever heard anyone say things like this? Are they true? Maybe you are thinking that, yes, most of the boys you know do try to be tough. At least, they do not seem to cry as much as the girls you know. And maybe the girls you know do seem to have better English grades. But then you remember that a guy in your class won the junior high essay contest when he was in seventh grade. And a male friend of yours seemed to be pretty much in tune with his emotions. So is all of this just garbage?

Let's state the obvious: there are some distinct differences between boys and girls, men and women. Although stereotyping is dangerous, the essential differences should be acknowledged. In the past, some people focused on the negative aspects when comparing the sexes. Using these distinctions to oppress or demean one gender is wrong and should not be tolerated. Yet the differences can also be viewed in a far more positive light. Try to see these differences as God-given gifts that make each gender unique. Each person has something special to offer.

Each gender's uniqueness is not limited to the obvious physical aspects of the bodies but also includes how they think—brain chemistry. Scientists are discovering more and more how brains affect the way people interact with one another, so it is all the more important to become aware of yourself and of members of the opposite sex. Social conditioning also has a role to play in how people relate to one another. From birth, your experiences have taught you how boys and girls should speak, respond to authority, dress, court each other, work, and almost anything else you can think of. Quite often in the past and even today, these societal conventions unfortunately have not favored women. It is everyone's job to fix this problem.

As you travel through your high school years, you will probably notice that girls and boys face different challenges. Girls must leap their own brand of hurdles and obstacles on their way to becoming women. Boys, who likewise must prove themselves on their road to manhood, will find that this road is paved with roadblocks and diversions that, generally, only boys will address.

Expectations for each gender vary as well. Some of these expectations are appropriate, while many others are improper. One of your tasks will be to decide into which category these expectations will fall. You will have to address the conflict you are going to face sooner or later (if you have not already), between what your parents expect of you versus what your friends expect of you. What is most important, though, is what your expectations are for yourself and whom God is calling you to become. What are your hopes, dreams, goals, and aspirations? Hopefully you will do this with guidance and assistance from your church, parents, and school, but eventually you must take responsibility and answer the question, "What do I expect of myself?" Ultimately your own expectations must rise above any others, especially those based on society's gender stereotypes.

In the end, your journey through high school will be infinitely unique. No one will ever go through your high school, in your time, in your shoes. Nonetheless, you might benefit from some observations regarding the obstacles and challenges your predecessors faced. This chapter will contain just two sections, but oh what important sections they are. In the following pages you will find:

- For Girls Only
- For Boys Only

NOTES

This section is for girls only, so, boys, skip
ahead to page 234.

For Girls Only

Charm is deceitful, and beauty is vain,
> but a woman who fears the Lord is to be
> praised.
Give her a share in the fruit of her hands,
> and let her works praise her in the city gates.

(Proverbs 31:30–31)

Situation

There you stand in front of the magazine rack looking for something to read during the upcoming family trip to Grandma's house. Experience tells you that this is a three-magazine trip. The covers of the magazines geared toward young women tout the following articles: "Ten Best Ways to Win a Man," "How to Have a Lean Body in Just Fourteen Days," "The Must-Have Accessories List," and "How to Use Your Horoscope to Have a Sexy Hairstyle." If that is not bad enough, models thinner than a lamppost and wearing outfits made of less material than your favorite pair of socks stare at you from these covers.

All you were looking for was some light reading material for a long car ride, but now you are wondering, "Are my calves too fat?" or "Maybe a tarot reading will tell me how to get Scott to ask me to the dance" or "Y'know, maybe my best friend is trying to steal my thunder! But what exactly is my thunder?" or perhaps the popular "I really would like to sparkle this holiday season!"

Before you know it, your venture to pick up light reading has turned into an all-out self-improvement plan that includes enrollment in a health spa, a new diet, and a self-esteem awareness program that will surely attract your school's hunkiest hunk. "Whoa!" you think. "I am too fat, too short, out of shape, and my self-esteem problems are hindering my ability to attract the perfect guy. I sure am glad I read this. Before I saw these magazines, I was perfectly happy with myself." Two months later you have three new subscriptions to these magazines and a growing list of items, traits, and experiences you never knew you needed in order to be happy.

How to Handle the Situation

To help remind you of the beautiful creation of God that you are, some excellent exhortations to elude the eradication of your esteem, as well as some other paramount points perfect for the feminine persuasion, follow on these pages.

 ### Real women are leaders.

- Since long before you were born, many generations of women, such as Susan B. Anthony, have demanded that they be treated with dignity and that their human rights be respected. In the big picture, it was not that long ago that women got the right to vote in the United States (1920). In many other places in the world today, the oppression of women is a cultural norm. Being a real woman means having the strength to stand up for what you believe and recognizing that you have dignity and incredible worth simply by being yourself.

- Despite the advances made by women in the past century, sexism is still a problem and, believe it or not, women themselves sometimes contribute to it. A real woman does not denigrate herself to become a mere object. A real woman has self-respect, integrity, and the acknowledgment of her own spiritual self-worth.

Be yourself.

- When a girl acts like someone she is not, people come to know her not as that "new person" but as a "fake." Your peers usually can tell when someone is putting on a show.
- When you try to act like someone else, you are doomed to fail. If you never let anyone know the real you, no one gets the chance to love you for who you really are.
- A fine line exists between putting your best face forward to attract friends or a romantic interest and trying to be someone you are not. Think about where that line is and do not cross it.
- Have healthy role models. Focus on who you are rather than what you want to look like. Who are the people you admire? Is it the model on the magazine because of

her svelte body, or is it your mom, a teacher, or another woman in your community who lives with integrity?

⚠ Do not compromise.

- Sometimes you should make compromises, such as what movie you are going to see with a friend, where you are going to eat lunch, and so on. Then there are things on which you should never compromise. These include moral issues and decisions that could affect the health and well-being of yourself and others. For example, your friend says that she will have just one beer before she drives you home. This is *not* an issue on which you should compromise. Or your boyfriend says that he will not break up with you if you have sex with him. This is *not* a question for consideration, nor should you compromise.

- Your actions reflect your character. Someone who does kind things is generally considered a kind person. Decide who you really are and let your actions tell other people who you are. Set boundaries for yourself to let people know who you are not.

- Plan ahead how you are going to address the difficult issues you might face in high school. How will you decline drugs or alcohol? Will you laugh as though they are crazy to ask? Will you blame it on strict parents who check up on you? How will you handle bullies? Yes, girls can be bullies too. Be prepared.

Dating does not have to be a priority.

- Dating can be a wonderful experience in high school. Playing golf can be a wonderful experience too. Do not feel pressured to date, and do not feel like you are missing out on something if you don't. Like golf, not everyone is enthusiastic about it. If you are not enthused about dating, do not worry about it.
- Dating can be fine, but it also comes with its own share of problems. It can consume a lot of your time and emotional energy. If you have other areas on which you prefer to focus (grades, sports, hobbies, and so on), you might want to consider putting off the dating scene for a while.

Save sex for marriage.

- Sharing yourself sexually is a deeply intimate experience that should be shared with someone you love and who has permanently committed himself to you (aka marriage).
- God's commandment to have sexual intercourse only with your husband is good spiritual wisdom as well as good advice for your health and well-being. When you engage in premarital sex, you risk the health of yourself, your partner, your future husband, and possibly even your future children.
- Yes, oral sex is sex. You can contract sexually transmitted diseases this way too.

⚠ Recognize an abusive or unhealthy relationship.

- Having sex with a boyfriend to keep him from dropping you does not work. Sure, it may work for a short period, but eventually the relationship will run its course. If a guy is pressuring you to have sex, ask yourself why he is in the relationship. Does he want to be with you, or does he just want to use you?
- If a relationship with a boyfriend begins to take up so much time and attention that your grades fall or your family and other friends are neglected, take time to rethink the situation.
- No one deserves to be physically mistreated. You deserve to be loved and respected. If you are ever physically abused or raped, go to a hospital immediately to get help and report the abuse to your parents, a counselor, a teacher, or another adult you trust.
- Emotional abuse is a lot harder to identify and acknowledge because there are no bruises or broken bones that someone can see. If your boyfriend is controlling, intimidating, overly jealous, too critical, insulting, forceful, or isolates you from other important people in your life, seek help immediately from your parents or a counselor or a teacher at your school.

⚠ Know who you are and what you are about.

- If you *really* know who you are, what other people tell you will not really matter that much. Fear and anxiety come when you think that what they have to say about you just might be right.

- Keep a journal. Take out a spiral notebook and investigate the goings-on of your inner and outer life. Make it a daily practice.
- Do not let your emotions control you. This does not mean you should suppress or ignore your emotions. Actually, it is quite the opposite. Become aware of them and acknowledge to yourself (or even to others) when you feel anger, sadness, fear, loneliness, and so on.
- Pray. Coming to know God will bring you closer to knowing who you really are: a child of God who is worthy of the love and respect that you will give to others.

Seriously, girls, this section is only for the boys.

For Boys Only

When I was a child, I used to talk as a child, think as a child, reason as a child; when I became a man, I put aside childish things. (1 Corinthians 13:11, NAB)

Situation

You are at home watching television and a beer commercial comes on. You see several muscular and athletic men on a beach surrounded by beautiful women. These young men smile and laugh as they toss footballs and Frisbees back and forth with the agility and balance of finely tuned athletes at the top of their game. One of them dives into the sand to catch a ball on the tips of his fingers. The images on the screen are tantalizing. They portray a carefree life of free-spirited hedonism, where guys with nearly perfect physiques relish gorgeous women and ice-cold beer.

Hold on. Something does not seem right here. This commercial is just wrong. Let's take an honest look at the life of beer-drinking. Someone drinking beer is actually more likely to

- burp a lot and have bad breath;
- not have the perfectly chiseled muscular features shown on these commercials but a healthy-sized beer gut instead;
- get dizzy and lose balance easily;

- say stupid and embarrassing things; and
- get arrested for public intoxication or drunken driving.

Hmmm. Does this sound like the kind of guy that beautiful women want to hang around?

Okay, the description might be an exaggeration. Certainly not all beer drinkers fit this description, but the portrayal is far more truthful than that of the muscle-clad ladies' men that the commercials present.

Take a close look at how men are portrayed in television shows, commercials, music videos, movies, song lyrics, and other places in the media. More often than not, you will find that men are generally characterized as sex-starved, incompetent, beer-swigging idiots who pay little attention to their families. No joke. Watch one evening of prime-time television on the major networks and you will see men portrayed this way. How many uninvolved or incompetent fathers can you count? How many of the men on the sitcoms are lame-brained blockheads?

Unfortunately this is a popular media depiction of manhood. The consequences are serious because many young males grow up thinking that these behaviors are not only acceptable but expected. Think about the consequences. These television portrayals may seem like funny stuff, but what is life like really for a son whose father cares more about staying all night at a bar with his buddies than he does about spending time with his family? What is it really like for a wife whose husband obnoxiously lusts after other women all the time?

Boys want to become men, but in this culture, boys often mistake the external for the real. For example, having sex seems to be a male rite of passage into manhood. After his first time, his friends might say something like, "You're a *real* man now." The drinking age in most places is twenty-one—an adult age. So drinking sometimes becomes a way to mark a boy's entry into manhood. The problem is this: these activities are *not* what turns a boy into a man. Consider the guitar. Anyone can buy a guitar, but the purchase alone does not make that person a good guitar player. Any guy can have sex, but that doesn't make him a man—because a man is someone who is responsible for his actions and respects not only himself but those with whom he interacts. In fact, when a guy engages in indiscriminate premarital sex, he proves quite the opposite: he is still a child. He is a self-centered individual who cares only for his momentary pleasure. He has no regard for his or his partner's health, future, or emotional and spiritual well-being. Does this description sound like a man to you?

So how is true manhood defined? One helpful place to look is the letters of Saint Paul. In these letters, Paul says that men should be gentle and not concerned with what other people think (1 Corinthians 4:12–13); not let lust guide their lives (1 Thessalonians 4:4–5); be willing to look foolish for the right reasons (1 Corinthians 1:18–25); support those who are weak (Romans 15:1–6); pray, be patient with all, and return kindness for evil (1 Thessalonians 5:14–18); and not brag or think too much of themselves (Galatians 6:1–5).

Admittedly, by our society's standards, Paul's man looks likes a wimp, but the problem does not lie with Paul. The problem is today's standards. In reality, the man Paul describes would be well respected. In fact, you might find a number of people who conform quite well to Paul's standards and who are also socially accepted. For instance, few people would deny that Martin Luther King Jr. exemplified the qualities of true Christian manhood as defined by Paul. Being a true man does not have to do with having power over someone or having sex or drinking beer or driving a car or (insert your own situation). It has to do with one thing: love for one another. Not romantic love or friendship, but what the Greeks called *agape*—selfless love. This is the love that compels a parent to jump in front of a speeding train to save his or her child. This is the love that requires sacrifice. Do you know anyone who fits this description?

How to Handle the Situation

Your road to manhood winds it way through high school. Many decisions lie ahead. You can make high school a training ground for an honorable life in which you respect your own person as well as those with whom you have relationships. To help you on your way, many means to mindfully maneuver your migration toward manly maturity follow.

Real men do not crack under peer pressure.

- Unfortunately, Catholic schools are not immune to all of society's problems. Sooner or later someone will try to coerce you into drinking or using drugs. Be firm and do not place your decisions in the hands of others.

- Be confident in your own decisions. Even your peers will respect that in the long run.
- Think before you act. Consider all the possible consequences for each activity in which you might participate, even the "unlikely" ones.

Real men respect women.

- Having a girlfriend around to hang out and have fun with is fine, but you need to be aware that it may be a much different matter for her. Keep her feelings in mind and be honest about your intentions.
- Using girls for sex, or just to have someone good-looking on your arm to show off, reveals only your own neediness and insecurities. Sure, maybe no one else knows about your insecurities, but you will.
- God's commandment to have sexual intercourse only with your wife is not only good spiritual wisdom but also good advice for your health and well-being. When you engage in premarital sex, you risk the health of yourself, your partner, your future wife, and possibly even your children. It is not just about you.
- Yes, oral sex is sex. You can contract sexually transmitted diseases this way too.
- Respecting women also includes resisting the temptation to view pornography. Pornography in all its various forms is demeaning. When you are tempted, it might help to recall that everyone, including women, is made in God's image.

⚠ Real men are honorable.

- Be honest in all parts of your life. Be honest with your friends. Be honest with your parents about where you are going. Be honest when you take tests.
- Work hard and be proud of the grades you get. If a C is your best work, you can hold your head up high. Cheating is dishonorable and an embarrassment.
- Cheating robs you of the great feeling that you did a good job. Even if done just once, cheating can taint your entire experience.

⚠ Real men are leaders.

- You do not have be the student council president or have any other official leadership position. Those are fine endeavors, but remember that there are many different kinds of leaders. Some are bold and outgoing, while some are quiet and simply let their actions do the talking.
- Do not be a blind follower. Peer pressure is just a way for your acquaintances to coerce you into ignoring your own conscience or good sense.
- Falling into the peer-pressure trap can get you into a lot of trouble. In fact, it can get you into a lot of things: detentions, car accidents, jail cells, even a coffin.

Real men know who they are and what they are about.

- If you *really* know who you are, what other people tell you will not matter that much. Fear and anxiety come when you think that what they have to say about you just might be right.
- Many famous authors, heads of state, and athletes have kept journals. Take out a spiral notebook and investigate the goings-on of your inner and outer life. Make it a daily practice.
- Do not let your emotions control you. This does not mean suppress or ignore your emotions—quite the opposite. Become aware of your emotions and acknowledge to yourself (and even to others) when you feel anger, sadness, fear, loneliness, and so on. Too many men these days act out inappropriately because they do not recognize or acknowledge that something is going on inside them.
- Pray. Coming to know God will bring you closer to knowing who you really are: a child of God who is worthy of the love and respect that you will give to others.

Acknowledgments

The scriptural quotations on pages 3, 10, 185, and 235 are from the New American Bible with Revised New Testament and Revised Psalms. Copyright © 1991, 1986, and 1970 by the Confraternity of Christian Doctrine, Washington, DC. Used by the permission of the copyright owner. All rights reserved. No part of the New American Bible may be reproduced in any form without permission in writing from the copyright owner.

All other scriptural quotations contained herein are from the New Revised Standard Version of the Bible, Catholic Edition. Copyright © 1993 and 1989 by the Division of Christian Education of the National Council of the Churches of Christ in the United States of America. All rights reserved.

The first quotation on page 51 is from "To Teach as Jesus Did: A Pastoral Message on Catholic Education," by the United States Conference of Catholic Bishops (USCCB) (Washington, DC: USCCB, 1973), pages 6 and 7. Copyright © 1973 by the USCCB.

The second quotation on page 51 is from *The Catholic School*, by the Sacred Congregation for Catholic Education, number 35, at *www.vatican.va/roman_curia/ congregations/ccatheduc/documents/rc_con_ccatheduc_ doc_19770319_catholic-school_en.html,* accessed October 27, 2006.

The quotation on page 97 is from *Declaration on the Relation of the Church to Non-Christian Religions* (*Nostra Aetate*, 1965), number 2, at *www.vatican.va/archive/hist_councils/ii_vatican_council/documents/vat-ii_decl_19651028_nostra-aetate_en.html*, accessed October 26, 2006.

To view copyright terms and conditions for Internet materials cited here, log on to the home pages for the referenced Web sites.

During this book's preparation, all citations, facts, figures, names, addresses, telephone numbers, Internet URLs, and other pieces of information cited within were verified for accuracy. The authors and Saint Mary's Press staff have made every attempt to reference current and valid sources, but we cannot guarantee the content of any source, and we are not responsible for any changes that may have occurred since our verification. If you find an error in, or have a question or concern about, any of the information or sources listed within, please contact Saint Mary's Press.

NOTES